NORTH DAKO'

MW01672257

Take the Adventure & E...

Fort Ransom & Beaver Lake state parks

INCLUDES Doyle Memorial State Park

by Scott R. Kudelka

Adventure Publications, Inc.
Cambridge, Minnesota

DEDICATION

To my partner and best friend, Angie, who inspired me to write this book!

To my parents, Roger and Shirley, who have always believed in me.

This book is for my niece, Jenny Kudelka Hanson, as she begins to explore and enjoy her own adventures in North Dakota.

Edited by Hope Klocker and Brett Ortler

Book and cover design by Jonathan Norberg

Photo Credits by photographer and page number:
Cover photo: Horse-drawn plow by Scott R. Kudelka
Angie Becker Kudelka: 29, 118 **Scott R. Kudelka:** 8, 9, 14, 15, 16, 17, 19, 20, 22, 25, 27, 31, 32, 33, 34, 35, 38, 39, 40, 43, 46, 49, 52, 53, 54, 57, 58, 59, 60, 61, 62, 63, 64, 66, 67, 68, 69, 72, 73, 76, 77, 83, 84, 85, 93, 94, 97, 100, 101, 102, 104, 105, 108, 109, 112, 113 **Shirley Kudelka:** 4, 5 **North Dakota Parks and Recreation:** 10, 11, 30, 36, 37, 41, 42, 44, 46, 48, 51, 53, 78, 79, 82, 87, 88, 89, 90, 95, 96, 98, 91, 92 **William Kincaid:** 36

10 9 8 7 6 5 4 3 2 1

Published by Adventure Publications, Inc.
820 Cleveland St. S
Cambridge, MN 55008
1-800-678-7006
www.adventurepublications.net

Printed in China
ISBN-13: 978-1-59193-182-9
ISBN-10: 1-59193-182-7

ACKNOWLEDGMENTS

Where do I start? Well, I want to thank and acknowledge everyone for the help they gave me in putting this book series together. First off, a big thank you to my family for their support, excitement and assistance with the creation of the North Dakota State Parks set of guidebooks.

I want to especially thank Doug Prchal and Donna Schouweiler with the North Dakota Parks and Recreation Department for their ongoing encouragement with this project and their support with the accuracy of the material. As I traveled across the state acquiring images, a number of people went out of their way to help me. This includes Henry Duray, Lorraine Schroeder and Dennis Clark at Icelandic State Park; Jim Loken at Beaver Lake State Park; Maureen Trnka and Dan Schelske at Fort Abraham Lincoln State Park; John Kwapinski at Fort Ransom State Park; Dick Messerly of Fort Stevenson State Park; Steve Crandall at Turtle River State Park; Larry Hagen and Bill Deming at Lake Metigoshe State Park; Eric Lang at Cross Ranch State Park, the staff of Lewis and Clark State Park, John Tunge at Lake Sakakawea State Park, and Dick Horner of Devils Lake State Park System. Thanks also to Erik Spencer, Mark Brown, and Kris Dirk for help with maps and photos.

Thanks to Kelly Sorge for providing material and photos on Indian Hills State Recreation Area. From the North Dakota Game and Fish Department it was Dale Repnow, Brian Prince, Bruce Renhowe, Dan Halstead and Craig Bihrle; at the U.S. Forest Service it was Darla Lenz; and material on the U.S. Fish and Wildlife Service was reviewed by Ken Torkelson, Jackie Jacobson, Lynda Knutsen, Ted Gutzke, Joe Maxwell, Paul Halko and Dean Knauer. At the Lewis and Clark Interpretive Center it was Kevin Kirkey. From North Dakota Tourism, I want to thank James (Scooter) Pursley for help with their photo collection. Thanks also to Kit and Fay Henegar of Captain Kit's Marina.

Finally, I need to thank everyone at Adventure Publications for giving me this great opportunity. It is an experience that will stay with me forever. Thanks especially to my long-suffering and dedicated editors, Hope Klocker and Brett Ortler.

MY PASSION FOR PARKS

I grew up in southeastern North Dakota in a town of 500 or so people. Forman sits on the edge of the Red River Valley, close enough to see the rich agricultural land but stuck with a rockier terrain. My parents enjoyed throwing us kids in the back of a cramped camper on a 1960 green Ford pickup in search of a new adventure. Some of our best trips unfolded within North Dakota's borders. This was a great way to explore our home state and experience the unique characteristics of a prairie landscape.

Author at Little Missouri State Park

Vivid memories of visiting state and national parks as a young boy still fill my head. The big trip of my youth was to the Badlands at around age eight, exploring a crumbling landscape where Theodore Roosevelt rediscovered his passion after the death of his wife and mother. In the various state parks, I pretended to be one of Custer's cavalry at the blockhouses of Fort McKeen, skateboarded along the rolling, curving roads in the riparian (floodplain) ecosystem of Turtle River and roasted marshmallows at Fort Stevenson Recreation Area before it became a state park. I also scrambled up the steep Pyramid Hill near Fort Ransom for a close-up view of the Viking statue; saw my breath on a cold morning at Icelandic and discovered aquatic life in creeks flowing into the Sheyenne River.

In the summer of 1986, I got thrown into the job of seasonal park ranger at Little Missouri Bay State Park, straddling the line between the Great Plains and Badlands. With no clue what this job was all about, I saw it as a once-in-a-lifetime experience. As the only employee of a 5,000-plus-acre park, this lifestyle charmed me and it didn't let go until the end of the century, when I finished my parks career as a full-time ranger. In between, I bounced around North Dakota working at Fort Stevenson, Cross Ranch, Lake Metigoshe and Icelandic. During that time I cross-country skied 104 days during the severe winter of 1996-97, helped build the Centennial Log Cabin at Cross Ranch and never took my service revolver out of its holster.

This book is a result of the work I did during my 15 years in the Parks and Recreation Department. A number of good people crossed my path in my life as a park ranger and played a major influence. Daryl Kleyer, a Sakakawea park ranger, took a chance on me more than once and gave me the job at Little Missouri Bay. Jesse Hanson, brother-in-law, mentor and the guy who introduced me to the Hensler Bar. Jesse and my sister, Lisa, always had a bed, meal and job when I was down on my luck. Doug Prchal was my late-night philosopher buddy and horse wrangler. Jim Loken, the one guy who believed I could soar higher than as a seasonal ranger at Fort Stevenson. Brad Pozarnsky, who allowed me to fly without boundaries. And Dennis Clark, Kevin Kirkey and Darla Lenz, three of my best friends, who were always willing to hear my stories and ramblings of life. To my brother, Brian, and my sister, Susan, who shared some of my best experiences exploring the state parks of North Dakota. Finally, to Chris, my other brother-in-law, who survived a chaotic 6-hour canoe trip on the Sheyenne River.

Author and father in the Badlands

TABLE OF CONTENTS

INTRODUCTION

You will find this quiet and scenic spot only by traveling one of North Dakota's many backcountry roads. Start your search in the southeastern part of the state along a peaceful and picturesque Sheyenne River Valley. One of the more interesting routes is on south Hwy. 21 out of Valley City. Or take the county gravel road on the northwest side of the river from Lisbon. The valley features winding roads among farm fields and stretches of forested and grassy areas.

Fort Ransom State Park is one of the best places to discover what the Sheyenne River Valley looked like at the end of the nineteenth century. This is a perfect way to explore an up-close-and-personal history of rural life and farming.

On most days visitation is light, including the summer season, and one can usually find a quiet, out-of-the way, spot. Visitors will be able to seek out a mature bur oak to pitch a tent under, hike along a challenging or fairly level trail and float down a meandering river. The 887-acre state park is considered one of the best preserved natural and historical areas in North Dakota.

Family enjoying a picnic

The park offers visitors a chance to ease themselves back into a time when the Sunne Farm was filled with draft horses and crops grew in the fields. Or one might check out the visitor center and learn about the area's history, then take in an interpretive program at the amphitheater next to the river. The outdoors type might hike the trails or in winter strap on cross-country skis for a trip through a hardwood forest. Equestrians have an opportunity to bring in their horses for trail riding and camping. And the fun-lover can grab a raft and float down the Sheyenne River on a clear, warm summer's day.

Fort Ransom State Park is at the crossroads of a wide range of natural, historical and cultural attractions. All you need to do is follow the Sheyenne River Valley National Scenic Byway, the first to be designated in North Dakota. If you go north you'll find Valley City and its 11 historic bridges, along with Lake Ashtabula. Or check out the village of Fort Ransom, just a couple of miles east of the park; it's a classic example of small-town America, featuring eating places, shops and lodging.

Driving toward Lisbon, visitors will find a relatively easy trip to the Sheyenne National Grasslands. A large swath of a tall-grass prairie ecosystem highlights the former sand beaches of Lake Agassiz. In between these well-known destinations are a number of lesser recognized natural and historical sites. This includes the King School, Standing Rock State Historic Site and the Sheyenne State Forest.

Sheyenne National Grasslands

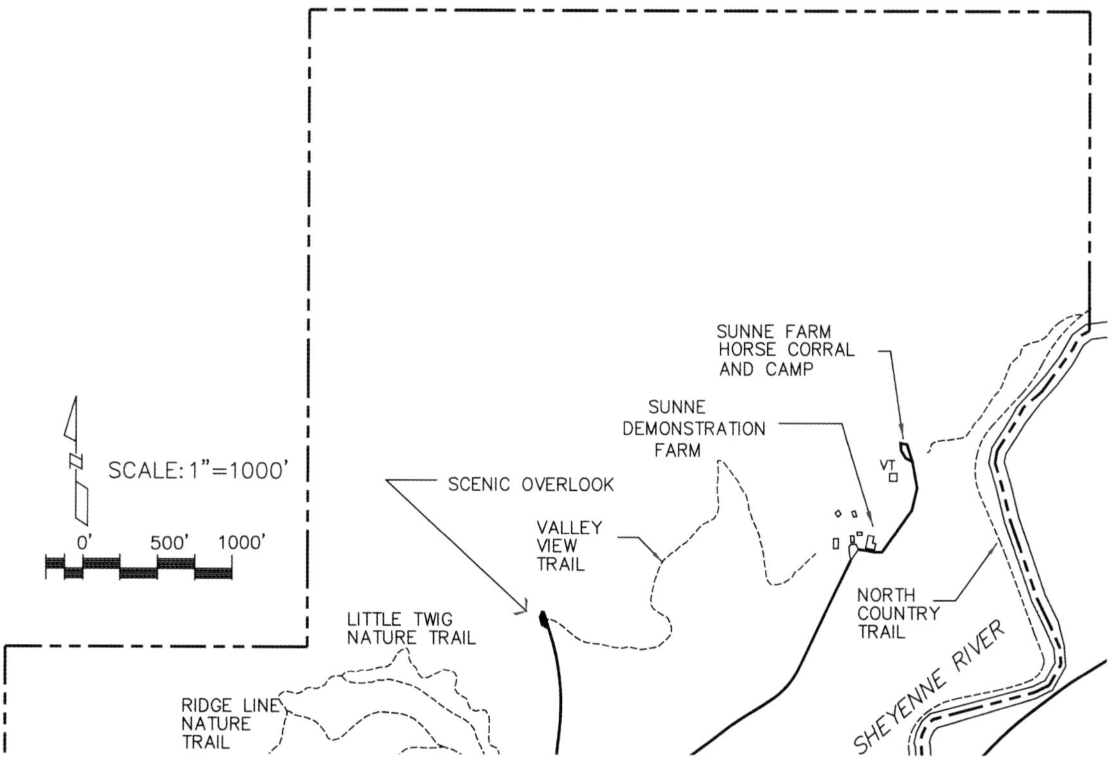
SCALE: 1"=1000'
0' 500' 1000'
SCENIC OVERLOOK
VALLEY VIEW TRAIL
SUNNE DEMONSTRATION FARM
SUNNE FARM HORSE CORRAL AND CAMP
VT
NORTH COUNTRY TRAIL
SHEYENNE RIVER
LITTLE TWIG NATURE TRAIL
RIDGE LINE NATURE TRAIL

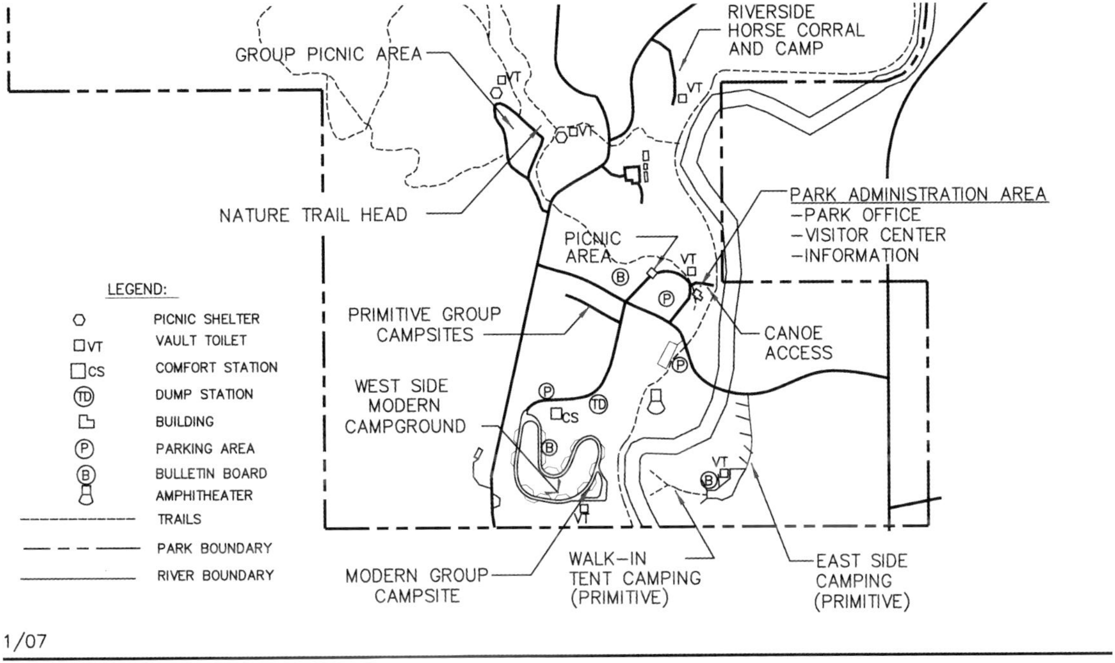
RIVERSIDE HORSE CORRAL AND CAMP
GROUP PICNIC AREA
NATURE TRAIL HEAD
PARK ADMINISTRATION AREA
-PARK OFFICE
-VISITOR CENTER
-INFORMATION
PICNIC AREA
PRIMITIVE GROUP CAMPSITES
CANOE ACCESS
WEST SIDE MODERN CAMPGROUND
MODERN GROUP CAMPSITE
WALK-IN TENT CAMPING (PRIMITIVE)
EAST SIDE CAMPING (PRIMITIVE)
VT
CS
TD
P
B
LEGEND:
PICNIC SHELTER
VAULT TOILET
COMFORT STATION
DUMP STATION
BUILDING
PARKING AREA
BULLETIN BOARD
AMPHITHEATER
TRAILS
PARK BOUNDARY
RIVER BOUNDARY
1/07

PARK AT A GLANCE

Location/Directions 20 miles northwest of Lisbon, 34 miles south of Valley City and 2 miles north of the town of Fort Ransom. A variety of routes can be chosen depending on whether you want to travel by pavement or gravel.

From Lisbon take Hwy. 27 west for 12 miles to Hwy. 58. Travel north on Road 129 (Walt Hjelle Parkway) for 6 miles to the turnoff for the town of Fort Ransom. Follow the Walt Hjelle Parkway to the state park.

From Valley City take Hwy. 21 (the River Road) south for 30 miles to the turnoff for the town of Fort Ransom.

Contact Information

5981 Walt Hjelle Parkway, Fort Ransom, ND 58033
701-973-4331; frsp@nd.gov; ndparks.com/parks/frsp.htm

Established 1977

Size 887 acres of bottomland and upper bluffs of Sheyenne River Valley

Visitor Services

- visitor center
- historic farmstead
- North Country National Scenic Trail
- special events and interpretive programs
- modern campgrounds, picnic shelters and playground
- canoe and kayak rentals
- meeting/kitchen facility
- horse corrals

- hiking, horseback riding and self-guided nature trails
- scenic overlook
- winter activities

Camping

- 30 RV and tent sites open year-round

Things You'll Want To Do

- Enjoy the park's modern campground, picnic shelters and playground and take advantage of the hiking trails and self-guided nature trails.
- Visit the Sunne Demonstration Farm and see how the pioneers lived in the 19th century; see a restored homestead house, a log cabin and historical horse-drawn farming equipment.
- Go for a paddle on the Sheyenne River in a kayak or canoe of your own, or rent one from the park and have it transported to the river for you.
- Drive the Sheyenne Valley National Scenic Byway and see the area's natural beauty from the comfort of your car.
- Bring your horses along on your camping trip, and go riding throughout the Sheyenne River Valley.
- In winter, enjoy cross-country skiing at the park and downhill skiing nearby.

GETTING TO KNOW THE PARK

VISITOR CENTER

The Bjone Visitor Center is filled with exhibits and displays on the history, geology and environment of Fort Ransom State Park and the surrounding area.

Open May 21–Sept 30

Rental Fee per day fee, (prices subject to change)

Facilities indoor kitchen/dining facility, tables and chairs for 64 people, vault toilets located nearby and modern restrooms at the campground or visitor center

Programs facility used for Sodbuster special events in July and September

SUNNE DEMONSTRATION FARM

This nineteenth century farmstead has been restored to show visitors how people lived and worked at the Sunne Farm. A number of buildings have been added by the Fort Ransom Sodbuster Association to highlight this agricultural lifestyle.

Sodbuster Building

This interpretive center helps visitors learn about the history of the northeast region. Here one can learn about everything from the glaciers that created Lake Agassiz to what it took to build a new settlement.

Sodbuster building

Sunne Homestead

Features home restored to the 1920s and 1930s era with period and historical artifacts

Programs used as an interpretive center and as a living history demonstration site during the Sodbuster special events

Sunne House

Machinery Exhibit Building

Features historical, horse-drawn farming equipment inside a 60' x 120' metal building

Machinery exhibit building

Homestead Log Cabin

Features accurate model of an early homesteader's home

Open during the Sodbuster events in July and Sept

Homestead log cabin

Picnic Shelters

Two small shelters are located near the Little Twig Trail head, just off the park's main road.

Facilities each shelter holds 6 tables; water hydrant and fire grills located nearby; volleyball court and vault toilets within walking distance

Reserve prices subject to change, contact park to rent

Playground and picnic area between Bjone House and picnic shelters

Picnic shelter

HORSE CORRALS AND CAMPS

Sunne Farm and Riverside horse corrals and camps are the two sites designed specifically for horseback riders.

Each area provides

- 8 pens, 15' x 15' each
- vault toilet
- water hydrant and tank

- fire rings and picnic tables
- manure bin
- pens can be reserved at no charge, 701-973-4331
- portable corrals may be used if pens are in use

Horse camp area

NATURE TRAIL

Visitors will find good entry points for trails throughout the park. At the trail head for the Little Twig Trail, there is water access and a bathroom facility, along with picnic shelters and a sand volleyball court.

CAMP AREAS

Five specific campgrounds are available for park visitors. They include the West Side Campground, East Side Campground, Primitive and Modern Group Campsites, and Sunne Farm Horse Camp.

NORTH COUNTRY NATIONAL SCENIC TRAIL

Many North Dakotans and out-of-state visitors are surprised to discover a national trail cutting through central and eastern North Dakota on its way to the East Coast. Created in 1980 by the U.S. Congress, the North Country National Scenic Trail weaves for 4,200 miles from North Dakota through Minnesota, Wisconsin, Michigan, Ohio, Pennsylvania and New York. As the western terminus, Lake Sakakawea is the starting point for the 475-mile section in North Dakota that stops at Fort Abercrombie State Historical Site on the Red River.

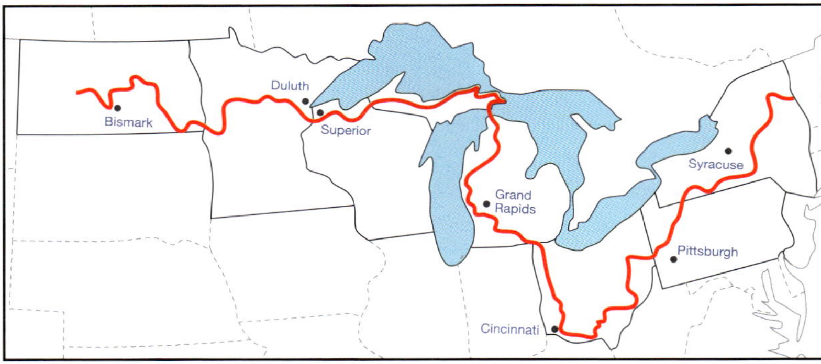

Map of North Country National Scenic Trail

The state's section of the trail features a number of significant natural and historical features. On the eastern edge, it crosses the Sheyenne National Grasslands before making its way to Fort Ransom State Park. From here the trail moves along or in close proximity to the Sheyenne River and eventually uses two unfinished canal systems managed by the U.S. Bureau of Reclamation. One of the more important natural sections for the trail is the Lonetree Wildlife Management Area.

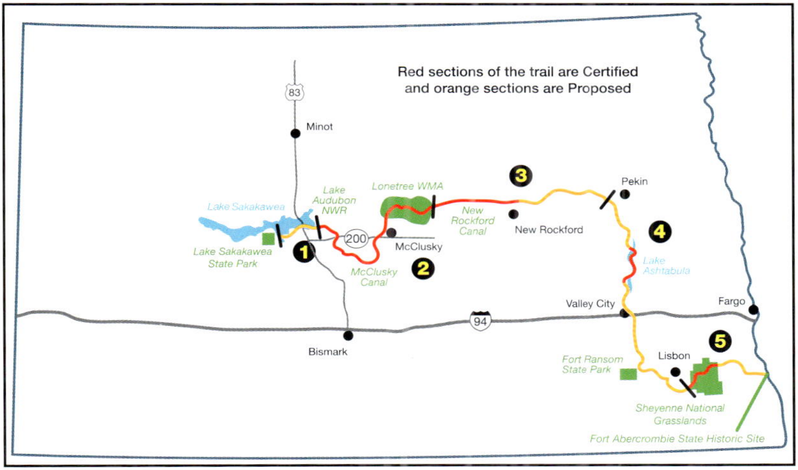

Lisbon to Fort Abercrombie trail map (section 5)

North County National Scenic Trail head in the Sheyenne National Grasslands

HIKING/BIKING TRAILS

A hike at Fort Ransom State Park allows you to walk through a variety of landscapes including shaded Sheyenne River bottomlands, steep blufflands and a smattering of native prairie sections. It is an ideal situation for exploring the plant and animal life of this distinctive river valley and enjoying picturesque views. Besides strolling along well-marked trails, you can also experience the beauty by mountain biking or horseback riding.

Little Twig trail

Riverside Trail (.3 miles)

- follow the Sheyenne River near the East Side Campground
- trail head located near the bridge
- no bikes or horses allowed

Valley View Trail (.7 miles)

- offers wonderful views of the Sheyenne Valley
- a variety of native flowers are found along the trail
- begins at scenic overlook and ends at the historic Sunne Farm

Little Twig Trail (.8 miles)

- one of the two popular self-guided nature trails
- begins near south picnic shelter and loops back to picnic area
- features a babbling brook and 4 bridges

Meadow Run (1 mile)

- originally a cross-country ski trail, now available for year-round use

Oak Ridge Trail (1.1 miles)

- branches off Ridgeline Trail, offering a gentler descent through open meadows

Ridgeline Trail (1.2 miles)

- one of the park's more challenging trails with a 250-foot change in elevation, but the climb is worth it!
- enjoy the view and catch your breath on a bench near one of two aspen groves

Sheyenne Valley Snowmobile Trail Segment (2 miles)

- a segment of a much longer trail that links Valley City and Lisbon
- trail enters park at its northern boundary and exits to the south

North Country National Scenic Trail

- following the west side of the Sheyenne River, this 1.5-mile segment is part of the 4,200-mile North Country National Scenic Trail, much of which is still under construction

Volksmarch (6.2 miles)

- park hosts the Fort Ransom Seasonal Walking Event from May 1–Oct 15
- walkers may register at the Fort Café in Fort Ransom, or at the park's visitor center

Trail Etiquette

- be considerate of other trail users
- watch wildlife, do not disturb it
- do not litter
- no motorized vehicles allowed on trails
- give audible signs when approaching other trail users
- keep pets under control at all times

Biking Rules

- please stay on established trails at all times and respect other users, including hikers and horseback riders
- yield the trail to all other users
- approach horses carefully, stop and wait for horses to pass, avoid sudden movements
- keep speed reasonable, prepare to meet other trail users at corners
- stay on marked and mowed trails
- Riverside Trail near East Side Campground closed to all bikes and horses

PADDLING

Visitors have a variety of options for canoeing and kayaking on the Sheyenne River. This includes putting in at the dock next to the visitor center or picking a section on the Fort Ransom State Park Canoe Trail. Experienced paddlers are encouraged to try the six drop-off sites ranging from 2 to 14 miles upstream and take advantage of the park's transport service.

Sheyenne River

The best time to canoe or kayak is in the spring when the water levels are normally high. By late July and August, during low flows, there are hazards including trees and rocks.

Beware of a lowhead dam in the town of Fort Ransom, about an hour downstream from the park.

- you must be 18 or older to rent a canoe or kayak
- park reserves the right to refuse to rent canoes/kayaks when paddlers are at risk

Canoe and Kayak Rentals at Fort Ransom State Park

The park has 6 canoes and 2 kayaks for rent. Each canoe can hold 3 adults. Paddles and life jackets are included in the rental fee.

Entrance Fee daily per vehicle or annual pass, prices subject to change

Rental Fees per hour, per canoe or kayak, for a minimum of 2 hours or a set fee per 24-hour period, prices subject to change

Deposit per vessel, to be refunded when vessel is returned undamaged; blank checks or driver's licenses also accepted as deposits

Reservations canoes and kayaks may be reserved in advance, but only for the entire day (prices subject to change); call (701) 973-4331

Rental Times canoes and kayaks available 9 am–7 pm

Transport Service Fees per vessel plus per loaded mile; no transport fee for putting in at visitor center dock

Drop-off Point	Distance	Duration*
Lyle Bjone	2 miles	1.5-2 hours
Myron Hammer	4 miles	2-2.5 hours
Wood's Crossing	5 miles	3-3.5 hours
Ralph Oehlke	6 miles	4-4.5 hours
Little Yellowstone	8 miles	6.5-7 hours
Kathryn Dam	14 miles	10-12 hours

**Duration depends on current, skill level of paddlers and rate of paddling.*

HORSEBACK RIDING

Most of the 887 acres in Fort Ransom State Park are open to people looking for a horseback riding experience. Riders will be able to explore off the trails, either along the Sheyenne River or the upper blufflands. Please stay out of the East and West Side Campgrounds, the family picnic area near the visitor center and off the Riverside Trail. All other trails in the park are open to horseback riding. Visitors are welcome to ride during the day or camp overnight.

Trails

Seven trails are open for riding: Valley View, Little Twig, Meadow Run, Oak Ridge, Ridgeline, North Country and the Sheyenne Valley Snowmobile trails.

Fees

- camping fee: per night, per camping unit
- daily horse fees: per horse, per day
- entrance fee: per horse, per day
- firewood: per bundle

Rules

- certified weed-free hay required
- if your hay and feed are not certified and tagged, they cannot be fed to your horses at the park
- park sells certified hay for per-bale fee
- any non-certified hay being fed to horses will be confiscated
- please stay on the Walt Hjelle parkway (paved main street through town) when riding within the city limits of Fort Ransom
- 3 hitching posts are located just east of Viking View Resort; riders are welcome to use these hitching posts and walk into town (provided by the Fort Ransom Arena Association)
- please stay off all other streets or alleys, along with the paved road from the museum to the ski area

Horse Corrals and Camp Areas

Two sites are designed for horseback riders: Sunne Farm Horse Corrals and Camp Area and Riverside Horse Corrals and Camp Area.

Each area provides

- eight 15' x 15' pens
- vault toilet
- water hydrant and tank
- fire rings and picnic tables
- manure bin

Reservations

- pens can be reserved at no charge, call 701-973-4331

Rules

- portable corrals may be used if pens are in use
- please don't tie horses to trees
- please clean up hay and horse manure before leaving

Note

Sunne Farm Horse Corral is closed during Sodbuster Days, which takes place on the second full weekend in July and the weekend after Labor Day.

Horseback riding in the park

CAMPING

Full service camping runs from mid-May to the end of September. All campers are welcome to use the comfort station and sewage dump station. Campground hosts are available at site 15 during the summer to provide information and assistance.

West Side Campground

- 15 modern single unit sites with pull-through gravel pads
- 1 modern group site (#26) with gravel parking
- 8 electrical hook-ups
- comfort station with showers and flush toilets
- sewer dump station

East Side Campground

- 10 primitive single unit sites with no water, sewer or electrical hook-ups
- sites 16-21 have back-in gravel pads
- sites 22–25 are walk-in tenting
- all sites have a fire ring and picnic table
- vault toilet is located between sites 20 and 21
- water hydrant near visitor center

Overflow Area

- used when all other campgrounds are full
- 6 primitive group sites
- fire rings and picnic tables

Canoe Campsite

- a single-unit primitive site
- reached by either canoe or foot
- fire ring and picnic table
- water and vault toilet at Sunne Farm

Horse Camping

- Riverside Horse Corral and Camp Area
- Sunne Farm Horse Corral and Camp Area
- must be traveling with horses to camp here
- primitive group sites

Reservations

- 1/3 of park's single-unit campsites can be reserved, call 800-807-4723 or go online at www.parkrec.nd.gov
- no campsite reservations at horse corrals, overflow area and canoe campsite
- modern group site 26, horse pens and picnic shelters can be reserved

Rules

- "Quiet Hours" are 10 pm–6 am
- campfires only allowed in designated fire rings
- do not camp on sites marked "Reserved" unless you have a reservation or have consulted a ranger

Enjoying a warm fire on a cool night

FISHING

The Sheyenne River is a popular fishing destination for anglers seeking walleyes, northern pike, rock bass and various non-game species. In May 2003, the river yielded North Dakota's state record common carp. The fish, which weighed 31 pounds, was caught by 8-year-old Austin Loberg of Thompson, North Dakota.

Favorite Species

Walleye

Revered by anglers for its sweet-tasting fillets, the walleye is a predator often caught early and late in the day, and at night, at the heads of pools and tail-outs of rocky riffles. A jig-and-minnow combination or nightcrawler on a slip-sinker rig is hard to beat.

Northern pike

A hard fighter, the pike is not as sought after as a food fish, but its fillets are good eating, especially if you remove the Y-bones. This toothy predator readily engulfs artificial lures and live bait. Look for it in slack-current areas such as eddies, oxbows and deeper pools.

Rock bass

Disdained by some panfish purists, the rock bass is nonetheless a strong fighter on light tackle and is good to eat—though its fillets are a bit more flavored than those of bluegills. Fish with worms, crickets or small artificial lures near rocks and gravel associated with vegetation.

Fishing Opportunities

Bank-fishing opportunities are abundant in Fort Ransom State Park. The Sheyenne's easy pace also makes it a great water to fish from a canoe, a small boat or a float tube.

WINTER

Even though it's a relatively quiet time, winter is an important season at Fort Ransom State Park. Snow and colder temperatures bring fewer visitors to the park and surrounding area, yet there are a variety of activities to participate in. You can bring the family or come alone for a weekend of fun or a few hours of solitude. Activities include cross-country skiing, winter camping, snowshoeing, sledding, photography and wildlife observation. Outside the park there is the Sheyenne Valley Snowmobile Trail and downhill skiing at the Bear's Den Mountain Ski Area.

Cross-country Skiing

A little over six miles of groomed trails wind along riparian, wooded, prairie and ravine areas throughout the park. There are trails for all skill levels from intermediate and advanced.

Skier on trail

At the trail head there is a warming shelter to rest and take a break from the cold next to a wood stove. Students from Valley City State College built this shelter.

To find out current trail conditions, check the ND Parks and Recreation Department website (www.parkrec.nd.gov) or call the park directly. Trails are groomed on a regular basis by the park staff.

Sheyenne Valley Snowmobile Trail

This snowmobile trail system runs from Valley City to the Sheyenne State Forest and over to Jamestown along a wide variety of landscapes, ranging from flat ditches and shelterbelts to the Sheyenne River and national grassland.

Snowmobile trail

More than 300 miles of well-marked trails are groomed regularly throughout the snow season of December through March. On the trail, there are warming shelters and a number of communities in which to rest and eat.

A portion of the trail passes through the park. These trails go through many private lands with access being gained by a lease through the landowner and Snowmobile North Dakota. The leases are essential to maintain this existing system. Please stay on marked trails.

Bear's Den Mountain Ski Area

Tucked into the hills of the Sheyenne River Valley is the local ski area, only a couple of miles northwest of Fort Ransom. It offers a chairlift, T-bar and a beginner's tow rope.

Downhill skiing in North Dakota

A modern chalet is available to grab a bite to eat, warm up and rent ski equipment. Ski instruction is also available, along with ski patrol for visitors' safety.

Hours Wed–Sat, 1–9; Sun, 10–5

Snowshoeing

This is probably the most accessible and easiest of all winter sports. If you can walk, you can snowshoe. Please stay off the groomed cross-country skiing trails.

Cutting across a snow-filled landscape

EVENTS/PROGRAMS

For one weekend in July and September, Fort Ransom goes back in time. Each year, the park holds Sodbuster Days, a historically accurate and exciting celebration of rural and farming life. The event attracts a wide range of people looking to step back in time to the beginning of the twentieth century. Other lesser known special events help a visitors explore the natural, recreational and historical side of the Sheyenne River Valley. Join a group of other visitors for a hike along one of the park's trails or watch how a 1870s-era cavalry performed military drills.

Plowing by horsepower

SODBUSTER DAYS

Return to a time when everything old is new again! Sodbuster Days are held to highlight and celebrate turn-of-the twentieth century farming. Drift back to an era when muscle and horsepower dominated everyday life at the Sunne Demonstration Farm. Celebrate this bygone era deep within the park, well away from visible reminders of modern life. Spend the weekend learning how hay is cut, smell pies baking over a campfire, taste the sweetness of homemade ice cream or get your hands dirty digging potatoes.

Held on Sat and Sun in mid-July and on 2nd weekend of September
Hours Sat 10–early evening, Sun 7–5
Cost per person fee; 12 and under free, or per family charge, (prices subject to change)
First Event held July 1984
Sponsored Fort Ransom Sodbusters Association and North Dakota Parks and Recreation Department
Activities planting, harvesting, crafts, ethnic food and children's games
Era represents the peak of rural life in America from the start of twentieth century through the early 1950s
Highlights live music, Sunday morning parade, style show, church services, food and beverages

Blacksmith shop

Demonstrations

- operating blacksmith shop
- pedal powered woodworking
- large, small and stationary engines
- wheelwright

- Valentine elevator
- horseshoeing
- horse-powered field work
- breaking sod
- planting crops
- cutting native grass for hay
- harvest and threshing oats

Threshing wheat

Ladies' Activities

- pioneer crafts and homemaking skills
- ethnic food demonstrations
- summer kitchen food demonstrations
- activities include cream separating, lefse making, ice cream making, weaving and spinning, quilting, fresh-pressed apple cider, soap making and jelly making

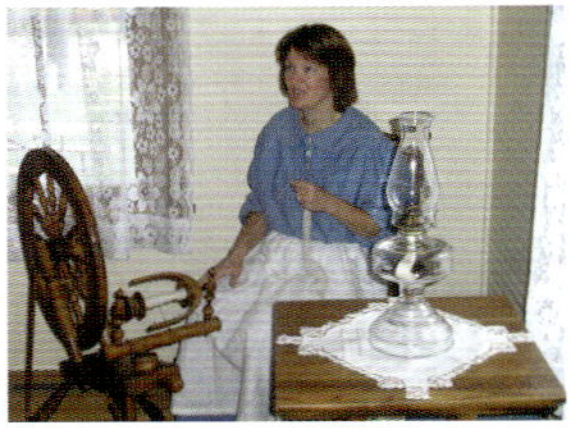

Wool spinning

Children's Activities

- watermelon seed
- spitting contest
- drawing contest
- storytelling
- scavenger hunts
- apple bobbing

Bobbing for apples

Farming

Corn, oats and potatoes are planted and harvested to give visitors a chance to see, hear, smell, feel and taste rural life. Visitors watch farmers use horses and steam threshers to perform vital tasks of an agricultural lifestyle and visitors are welcome to pitch in themselves. Horse-drawn wagons will transport you to the Sunne Farm, leaving the modern world behind.

Hay stowing at Sunne Farm

Food

There are plenty of hearty, harvest-style dishes to sample as well as Scandinavian delicacies such as Rommegrot and Lefse. Visitors can have a taste of homemade corn muffins, hand-milled corn, honey butter, hand-churned butter, homemade jams, jellies, fry bread and ice cream.

Pie baking

NATIONAL TRAILS DAY

During the first weekend of June, visitors can hike the nature trails with Park Manager John Kwapinski. In past years the hikes have focused on the North Country National Scenic Trail and the self-guided nature trails.

Come prepared to see a variety of ecosystems including native prairies and bur oak-dominated woodlands. Parts of the hike include challenging trail sections.

7TH CAVALRY PERFORMANCE

Come out to see the all-volunteer 7th Cavalry conduct military horse drills using authentic uniforms, equipment, tactics and weapons. This event is held on the last Saturday of September in conjunction with the Sheyenne River Arts and Crafts Association's Fall Festival at the town of Fort Ransom.

E Company of Lisbon will demonstrate parade formations, saber charges and weapon discharges. This reenactment group re-creates the life of horse soldiers during the settlement of the Dakota Territory.

Most of the equipment used is original or an exact replica of 1870s gear. Troops dress in authentic period uniforms and while mounted the unit maintains strict military discipline; they do not talk or motion while in ranks.

Additional Special Events

Also at Fort Ransom State Park watch for a Park Visitor Appreciation Day and an Antique Tractor Show. Contact the park directly or check out the department's website to see what other special events might be offered during the summer season.

Cavalry drills

Cavalry drills

INTERPRETIVE PROGRAMS

A variety of educational and interpretative programs are offered at Fort Ransom State Park on weekends during the summer months. They range from Dakota Explorer Programs for children to evening programs at the amphitheater and nature hikes. Check the weekend flyer or park bulletin boards for information on programs.

Creating your own craft

Dakota Explorer Programs

- for children ages 5 to 15
- activities range from exploring the natural environment to learning about the historical aspects of Fort Ransom and participating in cultural presentations
- participants receive a membership card, certification and other awards for successfully completing the program

Evening Programs

- traditionally held at the park amphitheater located in the Sheyenne River floodplain across from the visitor center
- look for special guest speakers talking about national wildlife refuges in North Dakota, the benefits of prescribed fires and the history of Fort Ransom
- held Friday and Saturday evenings at dusk

Nature Hikes

- park naturalist leads interpretive hikes exploring Fort Ransom's diverse selection of trails
- includes hiking through a variety of ecosystems from river riparian zones to restored prairie sections and upper blufflands of the Sheyenne River
- normally held on Sunday morning

NATURE

Located in the drift prairie section of the central lowland province, Fort Ransom State Park is characterized by a rolling, fertile plain broken by low ridges, shallow coulees, river valley blufflands and wetlands. The Sheyenne River is a dominant feature; it flows through a deep valley cut by glacial runoff in the Sheyenne meltwater trench. This landscape has been formed through the advance and retreat of glaciers during the Wisconsinan glaciation.

NATURAL COMMUNITIES

Forested sections encompass over half the park; the rest consists of upland prairie and former cropland. Managed as a natural and scenic area, Fort Ransom State Park contains a mixture of American elm, green ash and bur oak trees. A major prairie restoration has resulted in a flourish of native grasses, forbs and wildflowers. Visitors will also have a chance to observe a wide range of birds and wildlife.

Creek along Little Twig Nature Trail

Significant assets of the park include its high-quality natural communities including oak woodland, lowland woodland and mixed grass prairie. These increasingly rare areas are becoming more worthy of protection. Fort Ransom is unique due to its location as a transition zone where three major vegetation types converge: eastern deciduous woodlands, tallgrass prairie and mixed grass prairie.

Woodland Communities

Found on the dry, upper slopes is an oak forest dominated by bur oak. It has an open canopy, with few low shrubs and saplings. This ecosystem is commonly referred to as savanna-like in character.

Small woodland areas found in ravines and slopes leading down from the upland prairie are a mixture of bur oak and aspen.

Down on the bottomlands of the Sheyenne River is the Low Woodland community. Extending along larger creeks feeding into the Sheyenne, it is characterized by high moisture levels and is subject to flooding during periods of high precipitation and runoff.

American elm at the amphitheater

Upper floodplain hillside with sumac

Native Prairie

Original grasslands are primarily found on steep valley slopes that couldn't be plowed under, with almost no remaining native prairie on the uplands or fertile river bottomlands due to agricultural usage.

The greatest quality native prairie areas are found on the steepest slopes, often adjacent to woodlands. You will find both little and big bluestem, green needlegrass, porcupine grass, side oats grama, needle-and-thread, Indian grass and switchgrass.

Restored Prairie

Found in areas previously under cultivation for agricultural crops. These areas were planted with native grasses shortly after the park was established.

Currently it supports vigorous stands of native grasses with a sprinkling of forbs. In these areas yarrow, stiff goldenrod and pussytoes are found.

NATURE CHECKLISTS

The Sheyenne River Valley supports a number of diverse ecosystems and a large selection of birds, mammals and plants. Working your way from the Sheyenne River at the park's eastern boundary, you can walk one of the trails through restored tallgrass prairie sections and into wooded areas of the valley hills and ravines. Visitors will be able to experience different types of wildlife depending on the season and time of day.

Birds

One can't help but marvel at the abundant selection of birds found in the park and the varied types of habitats. One hundred and forty-seven species of birds have been observed in the park. Fifteen of these are on the Natural Heritage Program's state rare species list.

Pileated woodpecker

Here are a few of the many birds you can find at Fort Ransom State Park. See how many you can find!

- ☐ American kestrel
- ☐ bald eagle
- ☐ black tern
- ☐ Cooper's hawk
- ☐ eastern bluebird
- ☐ great blue heron
- ☐ great horned owl
- ☐ long-eared owl
- ☐ northern cardinal
- ☐ northern waterthrush
- ☐ osprey
- ☐ pileated woodpecker
- ☐ red-breasted nuthatch
- ☐ red-tailed hawk
- ☐ red-winged blackbird
- ☐ ruby-throated hummingbird
- ☐ scarlet tanager
- ☐ snow goose
- ☐ turkey vulture
- ☐ white-throated sparrow
- ☐ wood duck

Animals

Trails are top locations to spot wildlife in both the prairie and forests.

There are a number of animals at Fort Ransom. Try your luck at spotting them.

Muskrat

- ☐ beaver
- ☐ big brown bat
- ☐ common garter snake
- ☐ coyote
- ☐ eastern chipmunk
- ☐ mink
- ☐ moose
- ☐ muskrat
- ☐ northern leopard frog
- ☐ painted turtle
- ☐ raccoon
- ☐ red squirrel
- ☐ snapping turtle
- ☐ striped skunk
- ☐ western chorus frog
- ☐ white-tailed deer
- ☐ woodchuck

Plants

Ecosystems range from the tallgrass prairie to the riparian forest of the Sheyenne River. The type of plants found in Fort Ransom can be mind boggling, ranging from the bulrushes in wetlands to the giant American elm of the woodland community.

Check off each plant as you find it!

Native prairie plants

- ☐ American elm
- ☐ arrowhead
- ☐ basswood
- ☐ big bluestem
- ☐ boxelder
- ☐ buckbrush
- ☐ bur oak
- ☐ Canada anemone
- ☐ choke cherry
- ☐ Dame's rocket
- ☐ false Solomon's seal
- ☐ fireweed
- ☐ fragile fern
- ☐ green ash
- ☐ hawthorn
- ☐ Juneberry
- ☐ northern bedstraw
- ☐ pondweed
- ☐ purple coneflower
- ☐ sumac
- ☐ wild sarsaparilla
- ☐ yarrow

Dame's rocket

HISTORY

EARLY HISTORY

The Sheyenne River Valley and the Fort Ransom State Park area are rich in history. Prior to European settlement, a number of American Indian tribes made their home along the river or moved through on their travels. Once European settlers moved in, there was conflict between the two groups. Early in the 1860s there was a short but intense military presence, but with very little actual conflict. Eventually the valley was settled by a large number of Norwegian farmers.

Early American Indians

Mound builders, who roamed this area 5,000 to 8,000 years ago, were the first inhabitants of the valley. This group of American Indians lived in dugouts or semi-dugouts. Today you can still find these mounds of dirt, which were most likely used for burials. Inscriptions from these people are believed to have been left on a large boulder known as the Writing Rock.

High Plains Rendezvous, last held in 2004 at Cross Ranch

Several modern American Indian tribes later settled in the valley, including the Hidatsa, Mandan and the Cheyenne. All of them built earth lodges and traditionally followed an agricultural lifestyle. Each one of these tribes moved on to other areas as Europeans pushed into the state. Tribes such as the Ojibwe, Cree and Dakota passed through the valley as they crossed the Great Plains hunting bison.

Sibley Expedition

As the only active military operation to cross Ransom County, this troop movement was a result of the Minnesota Uprising in 1862. A number of

Dakota (Sioux) killed European settlers and burned their farms near New Ulm, Minnesota. The U.S. Army raised two separate armies to punish the responsible American Indians. It also included General Sully's troops moving into the Missouri River Valley from the south.

On July 3, 1863, General Sibley's army, on a western route, entered what is now Ransom County. Across this unsettled landscape a column of over 3,000 soldiers and an unknown number of civilians were stretched out for five miles. For eight days the army rested at Camp Hayes along the Sheyenne River (located downstream of Fort Ransom) waiting for a detachment from Fort Abercrombie. Despite their searches, Sibley's army never found the Dakota responsible for the uprising.

For more information, check out the Sibley Expedition of 1863 book *March on the Dakotas* by Susan Kudelka.

European Explorers

A Viking legend has persisted among some of the local historians for years as a way to promote a more complex history of the valley. According to a well-repeated story, a group of Vikings explored this area around 1000 AD. To support their theory these historians point out a set of mooring stones and remnants of a winter camp a few miles outside of the park. But who exactly were the first Europeans to explore the valley is still a topic of debate.

Pierre de la Verendrye led the first known European expedition through the Sheyenne River Valley in 1738. A fur trading industry followed in his wake, lasting until approximately 1860. By the late 1860s the U.S. Army had established a military fort overlooking the present town of Fort Ransom.

HOMESTEADERS AND THE BJONE HOUSE

Past

Bjone House, historical photo

Built in 1879, this simple 2-story house was home to a number of families over a century. Mr. and Mrs. Nils Olson built the home and were two of the first settlers in the valley. The house also served as the first church for the Standing Rock congregation.

Over the years a number of people lived in the house, including Israel Henrikson, Axel and Dina Skonseng, Bjorn and Petra Granlund and finally the family of Helen and Morris Bjone. This was typical for many pioneer homes. After a nasty flood, the Bjones sold the farm to the North Dakota Parks and Recreation Department.

Present

Bjone House today

Today the Bjone House serves as a visitor center, park office and meeting facility. It also contains exhibits and artifacts on the geology, history and natural resources of the area.

After the ND Parks and Recreation Department purchased the home and land, the agency started to develop plans for use as a living history farm. Unfortunately, all the outer buildings were destroyed due to disrepair.

The Lutheran Brotherhood funded restoration of the house (as a Centennial Project). Today, visitors can learn about the history of this valley and state park.

Historical Timeline

1879 Norwegian immigrant Nils Olson builds a pioneer log cabin. It is later incorporated into the larger house standing today.

1882 On February 23 the Standing Rock Norwegian Evangelical Congregation formed and services were held at the house for a number of years.

1903 Israel Henrikson buys the farm from Mrs. Olson-Eggan, who by that time was married to Nils Eggan.

1914-30 Elinas Skonseng, Helen Bjone's father, rents the land.

1915-22 Dina and Elinas have three children at the house: Arthur, Helen and Melvin.

1930 Israel Henrikson passed away in January and the Skonsengs purchased the farm.

1944 Helen and her husband Morris Bjone buy the farm in March. They raise four daughters.

1976 North Dakota Park Service purchases the farm, intending to use it as a living history site.

1989 On July 4th the Bjone House is dedicated as a visitor center and park office. It is funded by the Lutheran Brotherhood as a Centennial Project.

1995 Interpretive display panels are installed on the first floor and dedicated on October 14. Funds are again provided by Lutheran Brotherhood and the family of Snorri Thorfinson.

Memories of Helen Bjone

Helen's mother, Dina, came here in 1905 and worked for $1.50 a week doing house chores, taking care of Israel's parents and milking 19 cows.

Historical view of Sunne Farm

Over the years as many as 10 people lived with the Skonsengs, including Helen's uncle and a foster daughter. "They always gave of themselves and helped the neighbors with love, food, money, supplies and winter fuel," said Helen.

"When I was young, everything was done by hand or horse-drawn equipment; we walked after cows to milk them. We saw the change from horse to tractor."

The first car on the farm was a 1917 Ford Touring Car, which belonged to Israel Hendrickson. "We always had a lot of company and Dad made sure that everyone who stopped had coffee and lunch," she said.

Helen missed the solitude of her home the most. "I used to go for a slow walk in the woods and reminisce about what we've done, and what we're going to do," she explains, adding, "It was an enjoyable time to live there.

"We sold this farm to the Parks and Recreation, and our prayers and hopes are that we did the community a good and lasting deed. We hope that it will be enjoyed by people from far and wide, just as much as we enjoyed living in this area with all these good friends, neighbors and relatives."

Stable section of Sunne barn

SUNNE FARM

Originally homesteaded by Andrew and Johanna Sunne in the 1880s, the farm is now a living history centerpiece at Fort Ransom State Park. In 1884 Andrew Sunne emigrated from Norway to the Dakota Territory looking for a new life for his family. A year later his wife, Johanna, joined him; the two of them raised a large family on the farm.

An agronomist and horticulturalist in his native country, Andrew was mainly interested in experimenting with wheat and trees. Here in the Sheyenne River Valley he continued experiments in crossing different wheat varieties. Andrew wanted to develop seeds to be better adapted to the climate and soils of the area. His wheat test area was located in a plot south of the house. The children carried water by the bucket and hoed weeds while watching for rust and diseases.

Sunne also experimented with fruit trees to make them sturdy enough to withstand the harsh winters. Unfortunately, his efforts to bring peach trees to North Dakota failed. In 1912 Andrew Sunne died after contracting pneumonia on his way to Bismarck to show off his wheat.

Historical Timeline

1898-99 An addition is built onto the original log cabin. Shortly after Christmas of 1899, a fire destroys the interior of the house.
A log cabin once stood on top of the bluffs overlooking the farm. One of the Sunne daughters, Helen Libak, was born there and lived in Fort Ransom until her death at age 97.

1908 A kitchen, pantry and a bedroom are added.

1911 A granary is constructed.

1914 The barn is built after being shipped to Englevale by train. The lumber is carted by horse and wagon by Andrew's son. The Langners boys of Fort Ransom put it together.

1916 A garage is built for a newly purchased Ford car. At some point between 1914 and 1957, both the barn and house are moved. Originally the barn was located at the current site of the blacksmith shop.

1979 The Sunne Farm becomes part of Fort Ransom State Park.

1984 The first Sodbusters Day is held.

Today It consists of 14 buildings including the original house and barn, along with a number of demonstration buildings, a cook car, log cabin and two blacksmith shops. Sodbuster Days are held twice a year, in July and September.

Note

Norwegian farmers settled much of the Sheyenne River Valley near Fort Ransom. A deep-rooted Scandinavian heritage is still evident and continues to be celebrated. These new settlers were industrious and left an indelible mark on North Dakota's history. It resulted in a period of extensive agricultural development and homesteading. In 1882 Durum wheat was grown in the area, a first for the U.S., becoming one of the North Dakota's major grain crops. The Norwegians felt at home in the hilly, well-forested country.

PARK HISTORY

In the early 1970s the North Dakota Park Service, with the blessing of Governor Art Link, was looking to purchase land for a new state park. After the flooding of 1975 caused extensive damage to the Morris and Helen Bjone farm, they made the tough decision to sell. On September 29, 1976, the formation of Fort Ransom State Park began with the land purchase from the Bjone family. On November 10, an additional 80 acres was bought from Marvin and Solveig Nelson.

Park dedication ceremonies in 1979

On July 16, 1979, Fort Ransom State Park officially opened to the public. During the summer, dedication ceremonies were held for both the West-side Campground and a timber bridge across the Sheyenne River. The park expanded to its current boundaries of 891.7 acres when the state bought the Roger and Herma Redetske farm.

Crews from the Young Adult Conservation Corps (YACC) and the Youth Conservation Corps (YCC) assisted with much of the initial development of Fort Ransom State Park. These youth groups helped with projects including a 15-unit campground, a five-unit walk-in tent camping area, two picnic areas, a maintenance area, an amphitheater, a prairie restoration site and the park manager's residence.

During the 1980s a flurry of activity occurred at the park, including the formation of the Fort Ransom Sodbuster Association and the beginning of Sodbuster Days. Construction projects included the restoration of the Bjone House and a number of buildings added to the Sunne Farm. Fort Ransom State Park continued to expand with a national trail designation and a comfort station.

NEARBY/WHILE IN THE AREA

TOWN OF FORT RANSOM

The small, historic town of Fort Ransom was established in 1878, six years after the closing of the military post. Situated in a forested valley along the winding Sheyenne River, this community of 100 or so people celebrates its unique heritage every day of the year. Fort Ransom hosts a variety of events and activities throughout the year, often focusing on its rich Scandinavian roots. Go into town for a home-cooked meal, the mosquito spray you forgot at home or do a little antique shopping.

Ransom County Historical Museum

Listed on the National Registry of Historic Places, the Ransom County Historical Museum has an unusual collection of local and regional artifacts. Built in 1882, the museum was once a general store.

Location 101 Mill Rd. (NW edge of town)

Hours 1–5 Memorial Day weekend–Sept or by appointment

Contact 701-973-4811

Site consists of Ransom County Historical Museum, Barn and Flour Mill, Bear Creek One Room Schoolhouse and Pioneer Dam

Bjarne Ness Memorial Walking Bridge

Ransom County Historical Museum

Sheyenne Valley Arts and Crafts Association's Fall Festival

On the last full weekend of September, a festival of arts and crafts is hosted by the local community. Visitors will find close to 160 indoor and outdoor booths filled with a variety of products. The event attracts around 7,500 people each year. A non-profit organization, the Sheyenne Valley Arts and Crafts Association, offers a variety of arts and crafts classes during the year. For over a quarter century its mission has been to promote arts and crafts in rural North Dakota.

Arts and Crafts Fall Festival

Fort Ransom Stampede Rodeo

This annual event is held on July 4th at the Fort Ransom Arena. It draws thousands of people to watch barrel racing, calf roping and bareback riding. First held in 1959, the arena is located a half-mile north of town along the Walt Hjelle Parkway.

SHEYENNE RIVER VALLEY NATIONAL SCENIC BYWAY

As the first route in North Dakota to be designated a national scenic byway, the Sheyenne River Valley National Scenic Byway is a network of roads extending south from Bald Hill Dam to Lisbon. Celebrating the natural beauty of this area, the byway's theme is "Hidden Treasure of the Great Plains." Today the byway features 31 recognized historic sites pertaining to various moments in North Dakota history. Along the route, visitors will find cities of all sizes and a diverse selection of farmland and forested tracts. In the future, a Rosebud Scenic Byway Visitor Center will be constructed at Valley City and interpretive displays are being placed at recognized historical and cultural sites.

Fort Ransom from Pyramid Hill

The 63-mile, newly designated Sheyenne River Valley National Scenic Byway follows ancient Native American footpaths and pioneer wagon trails along this breathtaking river valley. Paved from Bald Hill Dam to Kathryn, it continues as a gravel road to Lisbon.

Contact

Valley City Area Chamber/Convention and Visitors Bureau: 701-845-1891

Lisbon Civic & Commerce: 701-683-5680

Fort Ransom Tourist Hotline: 701-973-4811

Fort Ransom State Park: 701-973-4331

Websites: www.hellovalley.com; www.byways.org

Lake Ashtabula

Formed by the Bald Hill Dam on the Sheyenne River, "Ashtabula" is the American Indian word for "Fish River." Intended to stabilize flows on the Sheyenne River, the dam was finished in 1951 by the U.S. Corps of Engineers. It provides water supply in drought years, flood control, wildlife habitat and recreation. Lake Ashtabula is 27 miles in length.

- supports large population of walleyes, yellow perch, white bass, northern pike and black bullheads
- variety of recreational opportunities year-round, including bird watching, fishing, boating, swimming, camping, picnicking, ice fishing and snowmobiling
- gently rolling landscape with a combination of grassland, woodland and shrubland
- 4 resorts, 4 camping areas with a total of 140 campsites, fish cleaning stations, boat rentals, restaurants and cabin rentals available

Valley City National Fish Hatchery

One of two federal fish hatcheries in North Dakota, it is operated by the U.S. Fish and Wildlife Service to raise game fish for stocking in waters across the state. April through June is the best time to visit this facility to see the operation of 13 fish rearing ponds. In summer you can take a tour during regular visitor hours. Other recreational opportunities include a self-guided nature trail with interpretive signs, visitor center, kids' fishing pond and picnic shelters, along with a canoe landing. Bald Hill Dam features another 20 fish rearing ponds.

Medicine Wheel Park

A reproduction of a stone solar calendar, the Medicine Wheel is located in Valley City. This large circle measures 231 feet around and has 28 spokes radiating from the center.

There is also an extensive Native American burial mound complex dating from the Woodland Period, which ran from the first through the fourteenth centuries. The park also includes scenic overlooks, woodland nature trails, an astronomy observation site and a solar system model.

Bridges of Valley City

At 3,860 feet long and 162 feet above the riverbed, the Hi-line Bridge is one of the longest single-track railroad bridges in the nation. Built in 1908 it is still considered a marvel of engineering.

It is one of 11 historical and picturesque bridges spanning the Sheyenne River in Valley City. Visitors can enjoy a walking tour of the bridges. Check out interpretive panels at eight of the bridges.

Writing Rock

This prehistoric site features inscriptions on at least two boulders, located on private land across the ravine from the Fort Ransom State Historic Site. Geologists believe the unusual markings, including script-like engravings, are either the work of ancient glaciers or running water. Local folklore says the markings were made by people living here 5,000 to 9,000 years ago.

Clausen Springs

This was the location of an American Indian encampment and council in 1853. The council was held to protect the tribe's treaty rights from non-Indian trespassing. The area is now a county park.

Purchased 1967 by Barnes County Park Board
Open May–Sept
Facilities includes paved roads, bridge shelters, comfort station, playground equipment, electrical hookups and courtesy dock
Activities numerous hiking trails and quaint wooden walking bridges

Creek flowing into the Sheyenne River Valley

Little Yellowstone County Park

It is often referred to as "the oasis of the prairie" and is a favorite picnic and camping area. It is well known for its breathtaking view of heavily forested hills and a babbling brook.

Location just off Hwy. 46; 20 miles southeast of Valley City
Open May to mid-October
Features offers miles of hiking trails, electrical hookups, vault toilets, wading pool, large enclosed picnic shelter, athletic field, a natural spring for pure drinking water
Wildlife abundant in park, including wild turkeys and bald eagles
Camping fees for tent, van or trailer, please self-register

Standing Rock State Historic Site

Known as "Inyun Bosndata" by Dakota American Indians, the Standing Rock is considered sacred. The 4-foot-tall Standing Rock is an inverted cone shape that stands on a complex of prehistoric burial mounds dating from the Woodland Period.

Standing Rock

Three of the mounds are circular, artificial hills in the shape of low cones. The fourth is a linear mound, which extends in a straight line. It is located east of Little Yellowstone Park, south of state highway 46.

Slattum Cabin

Typical of the earlier settlers, Theodore P. Slattum immigrated to Minnesota from Norway in 1870. Moving his family to Sheyenne Valley in 1879, Slattum built a dugout for temporary living quarters until this cabin could be constructed. Seven children were raised in the cabin, with two dying in early childhood. Today the cabin stands north of Fort Ransom State Park.

Slattum Cabin

Pyramid Hill

Looking over the town of Fort Ransom, this unique hill measures 650 feet long, 520 feet wide, approximately 100 feet high, and is level on top, with the north, west and south sides of uniform shape. Geologists consider this to be a natural formation.

Some people think the top one-third of the mound is manmade, built an estimated 5000 to 9000 years ago by an ancient civilization. American Indian tradition that holds this site is where their tribe first emerged on earth.

Throughout the Sheyenne River Valley additional mounds, stone circles and rocks have been found. Many have yet to be attributed to any specific cultural affiliation.

Thirteen mound sites have been identified from different time periods, including the Middle Woodland and Late Prehistoric eras.

Viking Statue

Erected in 1972 on Pyramid Hill just north of Fort Ransom by the Community Club, the statue stands as a symbol of the rich Scandinavian heritage of this community.

Viking Statue on Pyramid Hill

The project started when two locals, Snorri Thorfinson and Bjarne Ness, saw a need to promote the small town of Fort Ransom. Inspired by Snorri's enthusiasm for his idea that Vikings explored this valley, they put a plan in action.

Eventually Bill Woell, a Vietnam veteran, sculpted a Viking out of pipe and steel mesh. A helicopter lowered the statue into place on top of Pyramid Hill on the afternoon of September 26.

In 1995 strong winds damaged the guide wires and after a fund-raising drive, Todd M. Hoelmer repaired the statue.

Fort Ransom State Historic Site

In the spring of 1867, General Alfred Terry ordered Major G.H. Crossman to construct a 200-man post overlooking the Sheyenne River Valley at a point called Bears Den Hillock.

Interpretive sign of Fort Ransom

The fort is named in honor of Major General Thomas E.G. Ransom of the U.S. Volunteers, who distinguished himself during the Civil War.

Constructed to protect overland travelers and maintain order for the Northern Pacific Railroad, it was decommissioned five years later in 1872.

Location 2.6 miles south of Fort Ransom State Park on Walt Hjelle Parkway

Features remains of the post include building depressions and an 8-foot-deep, dry moat fortification

Contact State Historical Society of North Dakota, 701-328-2666

Sheyenne River State Forest

Located on the south side of the Sheyenne River, the terrain includes river bottomland along with deep draws and steep banks. Visitors can pursue a variety of recreational activities including hiking and wildlife viewing.

Sheyenne State Forest sign

Size 509 acres along the Sheyenne River

Location/Directions 10 miles west of Lisbon, 4 miles off Hwy. 27. Travel 9 miles west on Hwy. 27 and turn north (right) onto a township gravel road (122nd Ave). Due to a new bridge, vehicle access is now available from Sheyenne Valley National Scenic Byway

Facilities primitive campsites are available for hardy visitors; there is also a nature trail, with 1 mile certified as part of the North Country National Scenic Trail. Now a 2-mile trail leads to the only waterfall in North Dakota.

Activities fishing, canoeing, hunting, hiking, snowshoeing and cross-country skiing

Managed North Dakota Forest Service

Waterfall

Contact Lisbon Forest Service at 701-683-4323

SHEYENNE RIVER

A major feature to Fort Ransom State Park is the Sheyenne River, flowing along the east boundary of the park. Twisting and turning, this river is great for canoeing, fishing and watching wildlife.

Massive wall of roots

Formed by the melting waters of the Wisconsin glacier some 13,000 years ago, it makes for a relatively young river. As the longest river within North Dakota, the Sheyenne starts in western Sheridan County. After 581 miles it converges with the Red River at Fargo.

It is named after the Cheyenne, an American Indian tribe who once called this valley their home. The Cheyenne were pushed out of this area and later moved into the Black Hills of present-day South Dakota.

The Sheyenne is a narrow, meandering and generally slow-moving river. With a gradient of 1 1/2 feet per mile, the river drops nearly 800 feet from its headwaters to its confluence with the Red River. Throughout the year the river's flow can vary considerably depending on runoff and flood-control policies.

The best time to canoe the Sheyenne is in the spring or fall when more water is being released out of Bald Hill Dam by the Corps of Engineers. Normally the river will see its lowest levels in July and August. By canoeing the Sheyenne River you will get a chance to see a variety of terrain. One floats past rolling hills, wide bottomland forests, tallgrass prairies and rich agricultural land.

When glaciers blocked north-flowing ancient rivers, large lakes formed as the water backed up. As the lakes overflowed, erosion began to create the Sheyenne and the James rivers. Normally the Sheyenne flowed southward until Lake Agassiz's water levels dropped and the river changed course toward the east.

Eventually the Sheyenne cut across the muddy lakebed of Agassiz after it began to drain northward. At various points the Sheyenne and James rivers are less than 10 miles apart, separated by a continental divide. Moisture hitting the landscape across the two watersheds flows into oceans on opposite ends of North America.

Sheyenne River, always interesting and changing

Length 581 miles
Outlet Red River of the North, a few miles north of Fargo
Headwaters 15 miles north of McClusky in Sheridan County
Elevation Drop 800 feet
Age 13,000 years old, considered a young river
Number of Dams 21, the most of any river in North Dakota
Trees aspen, American elm, bur oak, cottonwood, basswood, maple, green ash and a variety of willows
Fish Species 53 known to inhabit river, about twice the number found in any other tributary of the Red River
Major Watershed Hudson Bay

Floating Down the Sheyenne River

An adventure on the Sheyenne River awaits anyone with a canoe or a kayak. As it flows across a diverse selection of landscapes, you never know what might be around the next bend or curve. The river cuts through wide bottomland forests, remnants of tallgrass prairies, productive cropland and rolling hills. A continuous mosaic of scenery creates the river's unique characteristics and beauty.

Floating on this lengthy, peaceful river you will find two large tracts of public lands, the Lonetree Wildlife Management Area and the Sheyenne National Grassland. Fort Ransom State Park, along with numerous small parks and public areas, is open for hiking, biking, camping, bird watching, fishing and additional recreational activities. You will have

On the Sheyenne River

the chance to spy white-tailed deer, squirrels, belted kingfishers, beavers and an occasional mink. A mixture of sand hills, forested sections and prairie areas will give visitors an idea what this valley once looked like.

A number of segments are highly recommended along the Sheyenne River for canoeing. It provides opportunities for canoeists of all skill levels, from beginner to expert. Please watch out for a variety of hazards including tree snags and lowhead dams. The following three stretches are highly rated for canoeing.

- Cooperstown Bible Camp to Thompson Bridge
- Bald Hill Dam to Valley City National Fish Hatchery or Chautauqua Park
- Fort Ransom State Park Canoe Trail

Cooperstown Bible Camp to Thompson Bridge 6 to 9 hours to paddle entire stretch

Access
- bridge 2 miles north of Bible camp
- bridge 1 mile north of Bible camp

- bridge near Bible camp
- Cooperstown Bible camp

  Note: The Bible camp is privately owned; call ahead of time to request permission to access the river (701-797-2174)
- bridge east of Bible camp
- Thompson Bridge

Hazards extensive snags from fallen trees require a few portages in the stretch north of the Bible camp. Watch out for low flows.

Flow Information paddling is usually best in spring or after heavy rains. Up-to-date flows are available on the USGS North Dakota home page: http://srv1dndbnk.cr.usgs.gov. The gauging station is Sheyenne River near Cooperstown (05057000). A minimum flow of 400 cubic feet per second will provide fair to good canoeing.

Kayaking the river

Bald Hill Dam to Valley City National Fish Hatchery or Chautauqua Park 5-8 hours
Access

- bridge downstream of Bald Hill Dam
- Valley City National Fish Hatchery
- Chautauqua Park in Valley City

Hazards Two rock dams must be portaged. Both are treacherous. We do not recommend canoeing through Valley City; there are several dams that would make the trip very hazardous.

Flow Information Water levels are dependent on runoff and releases from Bald Hill Dam. Check with the U.S. Army Corps of Engineers at Bald Hill Dam for flow rates and general river condition. The USGS gauging station is Sheyenne River below the dam (05058000). A flow of at least 80 cubic feet per second is recommended.

Contacts Valley City National Fish Hatchery, 11515 River Rd., Valley City, ND 58072-9619; 701-845-1891

Valley City Area Chamber of Commerce, 205 NE 2nd St., PO Box 724, Valley City, ND 58072; 701-845-1891

U.S. Army Corps of Engineers, Lake Ashtabula (Bald Hill Dam), RFD. #1, Valley City, ND 58072; 701-845-2970

Valley City Park District, PO Box 422, Valley City, ND; 701-845-3294

Fort Ransom State Park Canoe Trail 1.5 to 7 hours, depending on put-in point

Access

- Little Yellowstone County Park by Hwy. 46
- Fort Ransom State Park

Hazards occasional snags and deadfalls

County Map Ransom

Contact Fort Ransom State Park, 5981 Walt Hjelle Parkway, Fort Ransom, ND 58033; 701-973-4331

The park provides canoe rentals, transport, access, river conditions and flow information

Dams on Sheyenne River

Manmade structures of various sizes and functions interrupt the Sheyenne River at more than 20 sites. Bald Hill Dam is the largest dam and is at the lower end of Lake Ashtabula. It has the potential to store 40,000 acre-feet of water in the spring.

In addition there are 49 dams on tributaries and another 8 off-stream dams, totaling 78 dams having a major influence on the river's hydrological cycle.

Many of the dams were constructed in the mid-1930s and 1960s to provide municipal water supplies, power for grist mills and flood control.

Some were Civilian Conservation Corps projects and others were built for wildlife and recreation. Most are lowhead dams that store and impound little water.

Walker Dam

SHEYENNE NATIONAL GRASSLANDS

Known by the locals as the "Sandhills," this river delta is comprised of 450,000 acres of glacial runoff deposited at the mouth of the Sheyenne River as it emptied into glacial Lake Agassiz. Sand up to 90 feet deep can be found among 70,000 acres of federal grassland interspersed with 65,000 acres of private property. Today it is one of the last large parcels of tallgrass prairie left in the United States, consisting mainly of 135,000 acres of grazing land. Visitors will find a variety of low-impact recreational activities waiting for them here in the Sheyenne National Grasslands.

Directions 2 trail heads for the North Country Trail; 3 miles south of Hwy. 27 on Ransom Co. Rd. 54; 6.5 miles north of Hwy. 27 on Richland Co. Rd. 23

Recreational Options

- bird watching
- canoeing
- fishing
- hiking
- horseback riding
- hunting
- mountain biking
- nature studies
- primitive camping
- 25-mile segment of the North County National Scenic Trail crosses the grasslands. The trail is marked by blue diamonds.

Sand section crossing North Country National Scenic Trail

Cattle Grazing Livestock continue to be a significant aspect of the "Sandhills." The Sheyenne National Grassland supplies forage for the herds of approximately 83 family ranchers who are members of the Sheyenne Valley Grazing Association.

Wildlife And Plants

The "Sandhills" are comprised of overlapping ecosystems and home to more than 1,000 kinds of plants and animals. You will find species typically found in northern boreal forests, eastern woodlands and western prairies.

In wet years, tallgrass prairie plants tend to dominate and mixed-grass species flourish during drier times. Rare plant and ferns include yellow Lady's slipper orchid, lady fern, crested shield fern and the adder's tongue fern.

Aspens in fall color

This delta is home to one of the largest populations of the western prairie white-fringed orchid (threatened species) in the country.

Bur oak savannas are found on rolling hills and prairie wildflowers include prairie smoke, western wallflower, spiderwort, penstemon and hairy puccoon.

Once a common game bird on the prairie, the largest population in North Dakota of greater prairie chicken is found here in the Sheyenne National Grasslands. The male produces a "booming" sound during courtship and attracts females with its dancing. April is the best month to view the males displaying on their booming grounds. The ranger district has a blind available to watch this fascinating mating dance.

Bird watchers will find an amazing selection of species, including cattle egrets and pileated woodpeckers, along with songbirds such as warblers, vireos, meadowlarks, bluebirds, orioles and sparrows.

The "Sandhills" are critical habitat for two unique butterfly species, the Dakota skipper and regal fritillary. For a complete list of butterflies, visit the Sheyenne National Grasslands website.

Creek cutting through the "Grasslands" to Sheyenne River

Other wildlife to observe includes white-tailed deer, wild turkeys, coyotes, raccoons, gray squirrels, ring-necked pheasants and red-tailed hawks.

Along the meandering Sheyenne River, visitors will come across glens, springs, seeps and bogs. Forested sections contain basswood, American elm and green ash. In addition, North Dakota's largest cottonwood tree grows here in the Sheyenne National Grasslands.

The area contains the largest unconfined aquifer in the eastern Dakotas. It has a high water table, averaging only six feet deep.

During the drought and Dust Bowl years of the 1930s, much of the sandy terrain was devastated by overgrazing, lack of vegetation and strong winds.

Contact Sheyenne Ranger District Office, 701 Main Street, PO Box 946, Lisbon, ND 58504; (701) 683-4342

NATURE PRESERVES OF THE NATURE CONSERVANCY

On the Sheyenne Delta, a short drive from Fort Ransom State Park, two sensitive land areas are being preserved by The Nature Conservancy. The Brown Ranch Preserve and the Pigeon Point Preserve are located next to the Sheyenne National Grasslands. As a part of the larger Sheyenne Delta landscape of nearly 236,000 acres, the two preserves host a diversity of plants and animals.

Brown Ranch

One of the most recent land purchases in the North Dakota park system, the ranch is part of a river delta formed when the Sheyenne River once flowed into glacial Lake Agassiz. Most of the land has never been plowed due to the less productive sandy prairie soils. On the upland areas you will find plant species of the tall grass prairie, along with wetlands or wet prairies filling the lower-lying swales. The Nature Conservancy purchased the Brown Ranch in 2000.

Recreation Activities bird and wildlife viewing

Features

- more than 22 species of butterflies have been identified here, including the rare Dakota skipper and the regal fritillary
- a resident population of greater prairie chickens, one of the few remaining wild flocks in North Dakota
- the federally threatened western prairie fringed orchid
- other rare plants include dune ragwort, Bicknell's sunrose, upright pinweed and northern lady-fern
- prescribed burns have restored over 100 acres of disturbed prairie

Size 1,531 acres

Location 16 miles southeast of Lisbon

Directions take Hwy. 27 east from Fort Ransom State Park for about 15 miles. Turn south on 149th Street to McLeod. Continue on the gravel road out of town as it winds west and south for 2.5 miles. At the first

4-way intersection, turn west for 2 miles and then turn north for 1/10 of mile. The Nature Conservancy office is on the right side.

Contact Sheyenne Delta Office, The Nature Conservancy, 7290 146th Avenue SE, Milnor, ND 58060; 701-439-0841

Pigeon Point Preserve

To the north of Brown Ranch discover a diversity of wetland types and upland sandhill prairie. Visitors will find high quality fen (groundwater-fed wetlands) and shrub-meadow communities, along with associated rare plants. The Nature Conservancy purchased 861 acres and sold off 289 acres.

Recreation Activities bird and wildlife viewing

Features

- well-developed, spring-fed stream in the Sheyenne River Valley
- at least 15 rare plants found in the fens and wetland thickets
- 200 acres of former farm fields being restored back to native prairie
- beaver dams, which impact water levels of many of the wetlands and fens
- many bird species, including western meadowlark, yellow rail, Indigo bunting and pileated woodpecker

Size 572 acres

Location north of Brown Ranch along south bank of Sheyenne River

Directions Drive east out of Lisbon for 16 miles on Hwy. 27. Turn north on 147th Street and drive four miles to 63rd Street. Turn east on 63rd Street for two miles to a "T" in the road. Turn south into the preserve parking area.

RESOURCES

SUPPORT GROUPS

Fort Ransom Sodbusters Association

The Sodbusters is a local citizens' group formed in October of 1985 to celebrate their agricultural heritage. They strive to preserve this valley's culture by demonstrating farming methods and the lifestyles of their parents and grandparents.

The nonprofit group strives to turn back the clock and offer a taste of rural life at the beginning of the twentieth century. It has been instrumental in creating an educational living history complex.

Contact PO Box 56, Fort Ransom, ND 58033

Hay gathering the old-fashioned way

Historical Timeline

1981 Threshing show is held near the Kenneth Brock farm, just a few hundred yards southeast of Fort Ransom.

1984 In August the first Sodbuster event is held at Fort Ransom State Park to commemorate the 100th Anniversary of the Sunne Farm.

1985 Fort Ransom Sodbusters Association is formed as a citizens' organization. A 42' x 120' building is constructed by volunteers to store equipment and donated items.

1988 Association is incorporated as a nonprofit organization.

1989 Four Sodbuster Shows celebrate North Dakota's Centennial.

1990s Association members build a small engine building. Other projects include the addition of a small granary to store corn and oats. They also rebuild a cook car and move in a summer kitchen.

1998 Sodbusters build a log cabin and blacksmith shop.

2003 Awarded the Cal Renner Award of Excellence from the North Dakota Parks & Recreation Department.

2004 Recipient of President's award from the National Association of State Park Directors. The interior of the Sunne House is restored to the 1920 and 1930s era and dedicated.

Sunne House Dedication, September 6, 2004

NORTH DAKOTA STATE PARK SERIES

BEAVER LAKE STATE PARK

INTRODUCTION

"If I am elected governor of this state, I will build roads from all directions to the Park," gubernatorial candidate William Langer enthusiastically announced at the 1932 dedication ceremony prior to his election.

Stone pier on Beaver Lake

Beaver Lake State Park is dedicated to the early pioneer settlers of Logan, McIntosh and Emmons counties. It covers 266 acres and provides recreational activities including camping, fishing and swimming. Spread along a large glacial depression, visitors can reach the park from Burnstad on pavement or along gravel roads from the east.

As one of the oldest state parks in North Dakota, Beaver Lake is now known for its historical features including Works Progress Administration (WPA) structures, a former horse racetrack and caretaker's stone cottage. During its first decades, the park was a popular destination for visitors seeking a place to camp along the lakeshore or enjoy a picnic among mature green ash trees. After years of little improvement, the 1970s brought a number of key developments, including the construction of an amphitheater, picnic shelters, modern campground and nature trail.

Today the park is showing rejuvenation after almost closing in the early 1990s. One of the more recent major projects is the construction of two sleeping cabins, donated by a former resident of the area. On the nature side, Beaver Lake State Park hosts a variety of waterfowl and upland prairie birds. Check out the spring and fall migrations, when a large selection of ducks and geese can be found at the park and lake. There are also plenty of opportunities to camp, fish, hike, swim, picnic and just relax.

Venturing away from Beaver Lake State Park, a visitor can find both historical and natural attractions. To the southeast is Whitestone Hill State Historic Battlefield, an interpretive site from the Dakota Conflict of the early 1860s. To the southwest is the home of Strasburg's favorite son and musician, Lawrence Welk. To the north you'll find the Slade and Long Lake national wildlife refuges, both ideal locations for spotting wildlife. Only a short drive west is access to Lake Oahe, a reservoir on the Missouri River. And to the northeast is the large buffalo statue and Frontier Village in Jamestown.

Whitestone Hill State Historic Battlefield

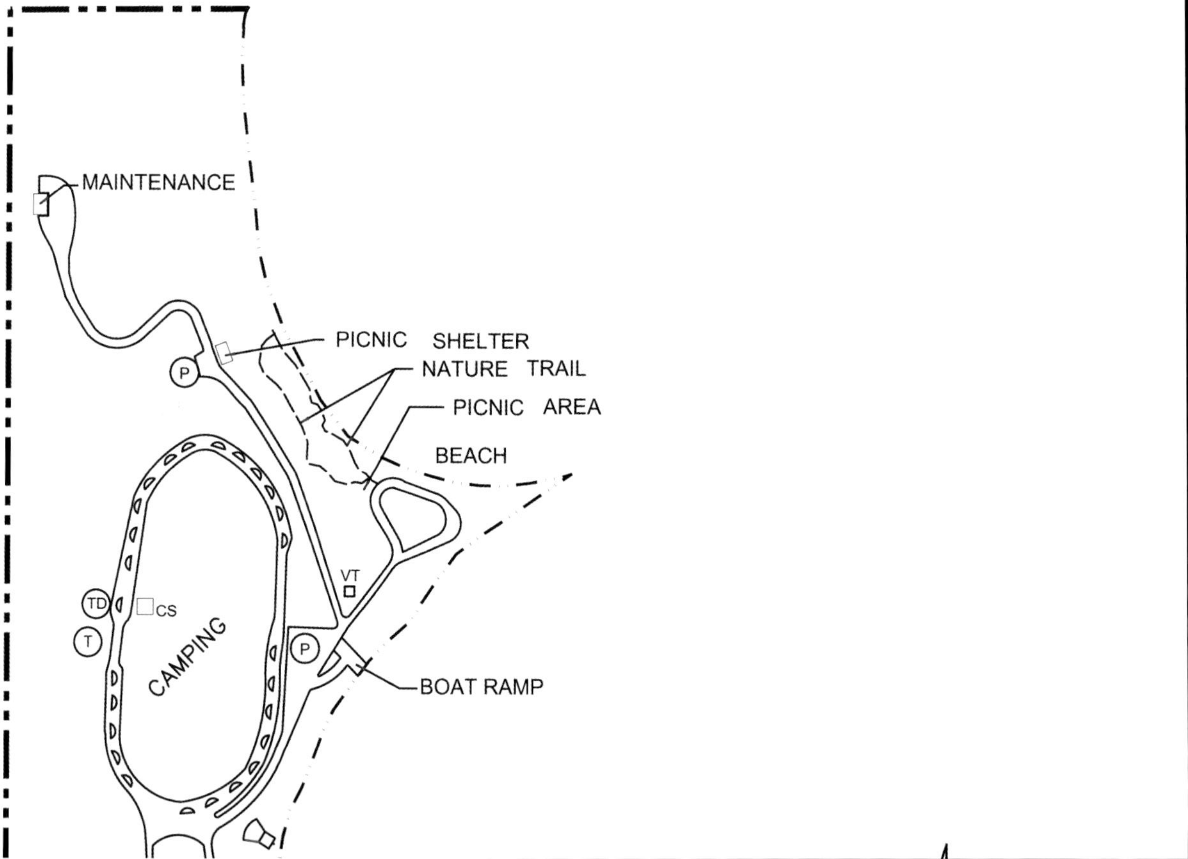
MAINTENANCE
PICNIC SHELTER
NATURE TRAIL
PICNIC AREA
BEACH
VT
TD
CS
T
P
CAMPING
P
BOAT RAMP

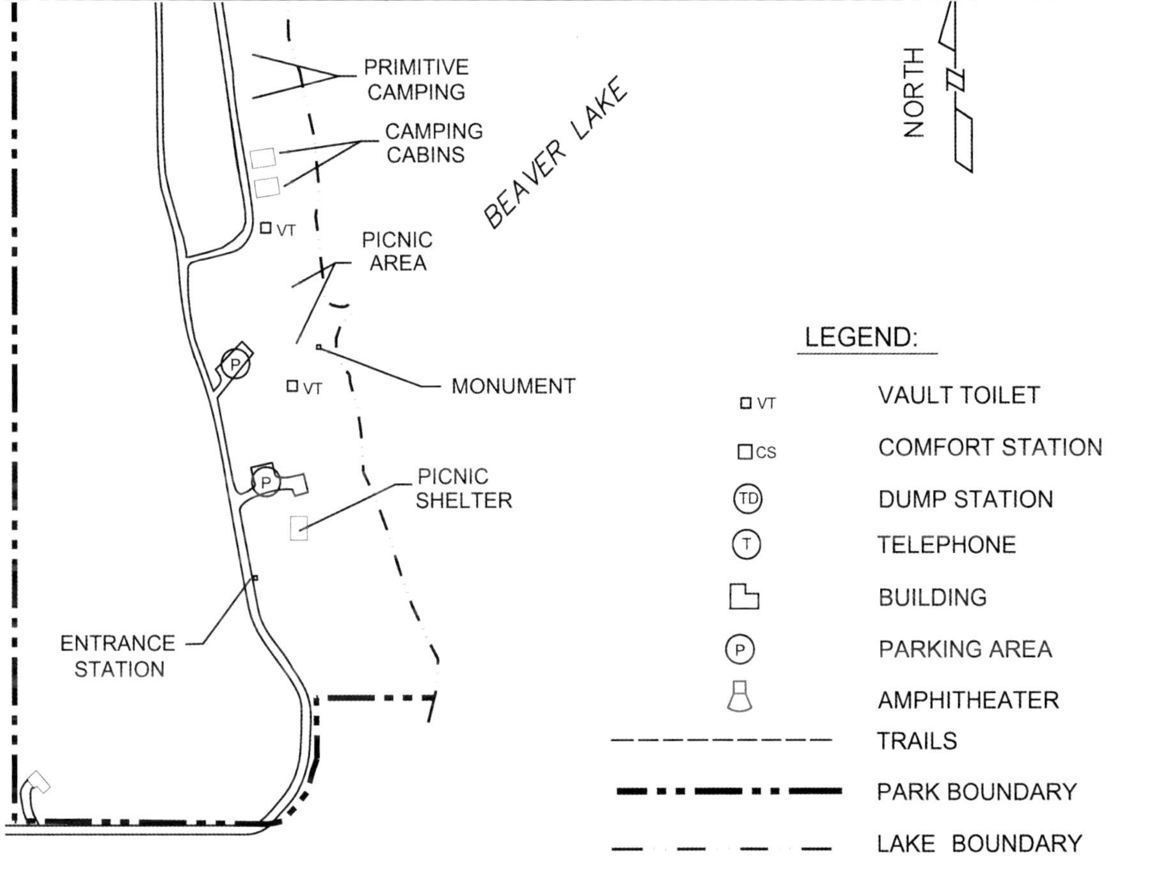
PRIMITIVE CAMPING
CAMPING CABINS
BEAVER LAKE
NORTH
VT
PICNIC AREA
P
VT
MONUMENT
P
PICNIC SHELTER
ENTRANCE STATION
LEGEND:
VT VAULT TOILET
CS COMFORT STATION
TD DUMP STATION
T TELEPHONE
BUILDING
P PARKING AREA
AMPHITHEATER
TRAILS
PARK BOUNDARY
LAKE BOUNDARY

PARK AT A GLANCE

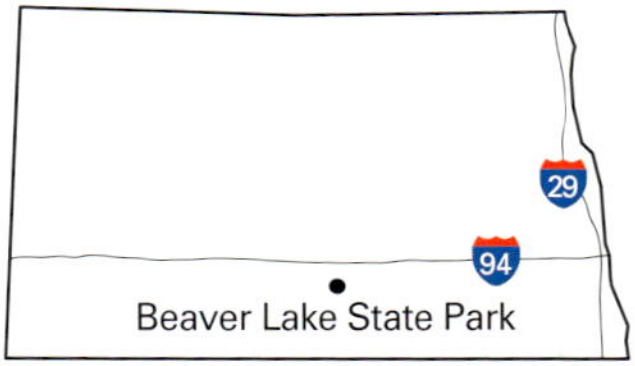

Location/Directions 17 miles southeast of Napoleon, 23 miles northwest of Wishek and 55 miles south of I-94. It is found on the west side of Beaver Lake, just three miles east of Burnstad.

From Napoleon, take Hwy. 3 south for 9 miles to 71st Street SE. Travel east for 8 miles through Burnstad to the park.

From Wishek take Hwy. 3 west and north for 17 miles to 71st Street SE. Travel east for 8 miles through Burnstad to the park.

Contact Information 3850 70th Street Southeast, Wishek, ND 58495; 701-452-2752; blsp@nd.gov; ndparks.com/parks/blsp.htm

Established 1932

Size 266 acres of rolling hills located along a large prairie pothole in the Great Plains

Visitor Services

- nature and hiking trails
- modern campground
- sleeping cabins
- picnic shelters, playground
- Works Progress Administration structures
- amphitheater
- special events
- weekend campfire programs
- boat ramp
- fishing
- swimming beach
- winter activities

Camping

- 25 RV and tent sites open year-round

Things You'll Want To Do

- Camp at the modern campgrounds, then enjoy a warm summer's day at the park's sandy beach and a meal at its picnic areas.
- Try your luck fishing in the lake, or go canoeing or kayaking on the lake.
- Hike on the newly created trails near the southern edge of the park, or hike on the nature trail near the beach area.
- Learn about the history of the Works Progress Administration (WPA) as you tour the park's WPA structures.
- Visit in spring or fall to observe the migration of waterfowl and other birds.

GETTING TO KNOW THE PARK

During the first few decades of the park's existence, Beaver Lake was best known for its horse-racing track. Though the races are gone, a remnant of the past is still alive today with the oval track road, now used for connecting each of the campsites.

Aerial photo of the campground and modern comfort station in the early 1970s

For years it was considered the fastest 1/2-mile track within 75 miles of Beaver Lake State Park. According to park history, people came from near and far to watch the races.

The North Dakota Park Service only owned half of the racetrack until 1950, when a land trade was made with George Lubbers to acquire the northern section for land west of the park boundary. At one time the track interior was used as a baseball diamond.

BEAVER LAKE

One of a number of medium-sized, spring-and creek-fed lakes that dot the rolling prairie farmland of south-central North Dakota.

Beach area

Facilities concrete boat ramp and courtesy dock located across from the campground. A swimming beach with a large stretch of sand is located northeast of the boat ramp. Go fishing for a variety of species including northern pike, perch, bullheads and carp.

TRAILS

Trails have been a part of the Beaver Lake State Park since its establishment in the early 1930s. In the last few years, a number of trail projects have been initiated to offer additional recreational opportunities.

Currently the park is developing a trail system through the south upland prairie section. Check out the self-guided nature trail and additional trails along the shoreline of Beaver Lake.

Interior of sleeping cabins

SLEEPING CABINS

- 2 cedar-sided cabins complete with foundations and furnishings were built with a private donation from a former Burnstad resident
- both cabins are located between the picnic area and amphitheater on the one-way road overlooking Beaver Lake
- each sleeps 4 to 5 people on a selection of bunk beds and features a refrigerator, a microwave, lights, heat, a fan and electricity
- large outside deck on each cabin is perfect for enjoying a nice warm summer night
- fire ring and picnic table outside

Sleeping cabins

- make reservations by calling 1-800-807-4723 or visit www.parkrec.nd.gov
- a per night fee (subject to change), also an entrance fee for all vehicles
- call the park for reservations

PICNIC SHELTERS

Picnic shelter

- 2 picnic shelters are located on opposite ends of Beaver Lake State Park, both overlooking the lake
- first picnic shelter located near entrance station and protected by west and north walls
- second structure found at the north end of park overlooking the nature trail, also features 2 protective walls
- walk-in picnic area sits between the south picnic shelter and sleeping cabins, also Civilian Conservation Corps (CCC) Memorial shaded by large trees
- each picnic shelter and picnic area has a number of picnic tables, grills and garbage cans
- contact the park for reservations

North picnic shelter and south picnic shelter

STONE PIER

Check out a stone/dirt pier built by a Works Progress Administration crew in the 1930s along the shoreline. It is located in the picnic area, below the sleeping cabins. Sitting along a wooded ravine, it is a perfect place to go fishing, watch waterfowl or enjoy the warm sunshine.

Stone pier

ACTIVITIES

CAMPING

- full service facilities open from weekend before Memorial Day to middle of September
- all campers are welcome to use the comfort station and sewage dump station
- busiest weekends are July 4th and Labor Day
- some campsites have excellent shade cover

Campground

- 1 oval loop near shoreline
- 25 modern and primitive single-unit sites
- one comfort station with hot showers and flush toilets
- 20-and 30-amp service available
- sewage dump station
- all sites drive-through and located on interior or exterior of oval campground road
- check out playground, horseshoe pits and volleyball court in the center of the oval

Reservations

- modern sites, (prices subject to change)
- reserve campsites calling 1-800-807-4723 or visit www.parkrec.nd.gov
- reservation line typically opens on first Tuesday of April
- please don't camp on sites marked "Reserved" unless you have a reservation or consulted a park ranger

HIKING

Nature Trail

- a self-guided trail runs along Beaver Lake through the northeast section of the park
- 18 stops along trail provide opportunities to view a diverse selection of natural and geological features

Nature trail

- pick up an interpretive guide at trail head or from park staff
- trail begins in the lake's riparian area and moves into the mixed-grass prairie overlooking Beaver Lake
- takes 30 to 45 minutes to hike and explore trail
- development of an extension of the trail system along the Beaver Lake shoreline is in progress

Hiking Trail

- 4-mile, single-track, non-motorized trail
- trail runs through the south upland prairie section of park
- hikers will find an accessible, gently rolling prairie trail adjacent to the shoreline of Beaver Lake
- trail head locations include park campground, picnic shelters and sleeping cabin area
- trail offers views of the rolling prairie that once dominated the Great Plains and ground-nesting bird watching—best time for viewing is spring

EVENTS/PROGRAMS

SPECIAL EVENTS

Some interesting special events are offered at Beaver Lake State Park during the summer season. Contact the park staff for dates and times.

National Trails Day go for an adventurous hike led by a park ranger on the nature trail skirting the shoreline and cutting through a mixed-grass native prairie. Starts at 10 a.m. at the trail head and covers various interpretive features. Normally held on the first Saturday in June.

Naturalist's hike

Annual Bullhead Fishing Tournament starting at 8:30 a.m. participants of all ages compete in a friendly tourney with both children and adult divisions. There are cash prizes, an interpretive program and special appearance by Roscoe Raccoon, the North Dakota State Parks mascot. It is traditionally held on Father's Day, a special free fishing day for children under the age of 15.

Visitor Appreciation Day entrance fee is waived on Father's Day to thank the community and visitors for their support of the park. Come out to Beaver Lake for a family fun adventure.

INTERPRETIVE PROGRAMS

- offered on a special basis throughout summer, programs include guest speakers, children's activities, along with nature documentaries
- check with park staff or at the bulletin boards for a schedule of programs and events

Amphitheater program

NATURE

Sitting along a lake carved from glaciers thousands of years ago, Beaver Lake State Park is part of the Great Plains terrain. A mixed-grass prairie dominated this rolling landscape before the advent of the sod-breaking pioneer farmers. Today the lake is well-known for its bird watching opportunities, including a diverse selection of waterfowl. Check out remnants of the glacial era, former prairie characteristics and a lake riparian ecosystem. For an ideal place to get in touch with the natural elements, go for a hike on the park's nature trail.

GEOLOGY

The landscape of Beaver Lake State Park was created by glaciers pushing out of the north, bringing along large amounts of rock and soil. Today you will find remnants of these ice packs in the form of boulders carried down from Canada, and of course, prairie potholes.

Glaciers covered parts of North Dakota for thousands of years, with the last glaciation episode occurring from 700,000 to 10,000 years ago. Receding northward, it left behind a layer of gravel, sand, silt and clay.

Beaver Lake, picnic shelter and rolling terrain

BEAVER LAKE

Glaciers pushing southward scraped out this depression in the rolling landscape. Nearly 12,000 years ago, melting ice filled Beaver Lake, in addition to leaving behind rock and gravel.

One of the largest bodies of water in the southern part of the state, Beaver Lake is around three miles in length north to south and has an average width of about three-fourths of a mile. Classified as a shallow lake, it is fed by Little Beaver Creek at the southern end, plus numerous springs along the northwest and eastern shorelines. Big Beaver Creek flows out of the lake in a southwesterly direction toward the Missouri River.

Today the lake is an important resting and nesting area for migratory waterfowl and other birds, including white pelicans, mallard ducks and Canada geese. Also look for grebes, cormorants, whistling swans, hawks, herons, bitterns, sandpipers, gulls, terns, kingbirds, warblers and goldfinches.

Beaver Lake

MIXED-GRASS PRAIRIE

Beaver Lake straddles the transitional line between the eastern tallgrass prairie and western shortgrass prairie, bringing a mixture of the two ecosystems together. In this mixed-grass landscape you will find a number of grasses, flowers and forbs from each of the ecosystems.

Little bluestem

Check out depressions and ravines for moisture-loving plants such as big bluestem, needle-and-thread, western wheatgrass and others. On the drier rolling hillsides, short grasses will be found, including little bluestem, blue grama and side-oats grama.

A variety of native flowers and forbs can also be found throughout the park. Some you will find fairly easily, including purple coneflower, yellow coneflower, blazing star and stiff sunflower.

The woody riparian areas and grasslands provide habitat for a variety of wildlife such as porcupines, white-tailed deer, raccoons, badgers, voles and pocket gophers.

NATURE CHECKLISTS

The interior of North Dakota is one of most important migrating routes and nesting areas for waterfowl in North America. Beaver Lake is one of many bodies of water found throughout the prairie pothole region attracting a wide range of ducks, geese and other water birds such as double-crested cormorants. A combination of wooded shoreline and native prairie provides food and shelter for many types of birds and other wildlife.

Birds

Visitors will be able to spot an interesting variety of waterfowl and upland prairie birds.

- ☐ blue-winged teal
- ☐ Canada goose
- ☐ cattle egret
- ☐ double-crested cormorant
- ☐ eastern kingbird
- ☐ western kingbird
- ☐ Forster's tern
- ☐ Franklin's gull
- ☐ goldfinch
- ☐ gray partridge
- ☐ mallard duck
- ☐ pintail
- ☐ red-tailed hawk
- ☐ ring-necked pheasant
- ☐ sandhill crane
- ☐ sharp-tailed grouse
- ☐ warbler
- ☐ whistling swan
- ☐ white pelican
- ☐ whooping crane

The double-crested cormorant, a large, all-black bird, likes to perch on branches to dry off in the sun, usually with its wings open. You will be able to identify the bird by its long, snake-like neck and long yellow-orange bill with a hooked tip.

Double-crested cormorants

NATURE

Mammals

The forested areas and native prairie provide habitat for a wide variety of wildlife both large and small. Take a walk on the nature trail for good viewing opportunities at dawn and dusk. See which animals you can spot!

- ☐ badger
- ☐ beaver
- ☐ coyote
- ☐ deer mouse
- ☐ Franklin's ground squirrel
- ☐ mink
- ☐ muskrat
- ☐ pocket gopher
- ☐ red fox
- ☐ striped skunk
- ☐ 13-lined ground squirrel
- ☐ vole
- ☐ white-tailed deer

Beavers are the second-largest rodent in the world—an adult can weigh 35 to 65 pounds. Look for its distinctive V-wake when swimming and for gnawed-down trees along the shoreline. The beaver is almost a completely aquatic animal.

Beaver on shoreline

Plants

Beaver Lake State Park falls into two major ecosystems—a forested riparian zone and native prairie terrain. Go for a walk on the nature trail to get a close-up view of both worlds. This is a transition zone between the tall-grass and shortgrass prairies. Check off each plant as you find it!

Spiderwort

- ☐ American plum
- ☐ big bluestem
- ☐ blazing star
- ☐ buckbrush
- ☐ choke cherry
- ☐ common milkweed
- ☐ cottonwood
- ☐ false dandelion
- ☐ golden currant
- ☐ hawthorn
- ☐ leadplant
- ☐ needle-and-thread
- ☐ pasque flower
- ☐ pasture sage
- ☐ poison ivy
- ☐ red osier dogwood
- ☐ Russian olive
- ☐ sand cherry
- ☐ stinging nettle
- ☐ wild columbine
- ☐ wild rose
- ☐ Wood's rose
- ☐ yellow sweet clover
- ☐ yucca

HISTORY

One of the oldest state parks in North Dakota, Beaver Lake was created by local residents to celebrate the original pioneers of the area and was first developed during the Great Depression. This large prairie pothole was a popular spot for camping, picnicking, fishing, swimming and a variety of additional activities during the first few decades of existence. Beaver Lake State Park became well-known for its oval race track, attracting large crowds from a 70-plus-mile radius. Today the park is enjoying resurgence in visitation due to improvement of facilities.

THE BEGINNING AND THE WORKS PROGRESS ADMINISTRATION

An informal meeting of local residents July 14, 1929 became the first step in the establishment of Beaver Lake State Park. Held at Shepard's Pavilion, south of the original park boundaries, it led to an organized effort to honor the early settlers living along the lake.

Civilian Conservation Corps (CCC) Stone Monument

Two lots in section 21 were bought for $1,437 in August of 1930 and work began on developing Beaver Lake State Park. Originally, lots within the park were sold to raise money for construction of facilities. On July 24, 1932 dedication ceremonies were held in the newly created state park, attracting between 2,000 and 3,000 people.

Despite the ongoing devastation of drought and Depression, the 1930s proved to be a boost for park development and visitation. For a number of years, crews from the Works Progress Administration (WPA) improved the park by building roads, a fishing pier, a stone monument, a bathhouse and terraced picnic areas.

The 1930s also saw a dam built on Big Beaver Creek to raise the level of the lake to improve fishing. A stone cottage was built by O.F. Arntz near the park entrance and later used by caretakers. In addition, businessmen from Burnstad built a refreshment stand to raise money for park development.

By the park's 20th anniversary in 1952, Beaver Lake State Park had grown to 125 acres from an original size of 45 acres. Features of the park included the fastest 1/2-mile horse race track within seventy-five miles and a baseball diamond inside the course. There was also playground equipment, a boat dock and electricity for the low price of $48 a year. The park hosted a number of annual events including Old Settlers' Day and Park Day.

Park welcome sign

HISTORY

1970s & 1980s

Modern campground

Beaver Lake State Park enjoyed a decade of focus by the North Dakota Parks and Recreation Department before becoming a seasonally operated facility. The state took over management of the park from a local group in 1972 and built a modern campground the next year, utilizing the former racetrack. In 1975, the first park manager was assigned to Beaver Lake and a manager's residence was constructed. During this time, a major land acquisition took place with the purchase of the Hoberg property and a 3-story house.

The last full-time employee transferred out in 1988 and by 1991 it looked like Beaver Lake State Park might close due to budget cutbacks. Fortunately, the local community came together to provide their support for this important local feature. Today the park is enjoying a renewal in visitation and recently saw the construction of two sleeping cabins.

Beaver Lake is now staffed by a full-time park manager whose responsibilities include development of a handicapped accessible comfort station and improving the trail system.

Entrance station

NEARBY/WHILE IN THE AREA

LONG LAKE NATIONAL WILDLIFE REFUGE

Designated as a Globally Important Bird Area and Western Hemisphere Shorebird Reserve Network Site, this rolling prairie and wetland complex hosts a large selection of migrating birds.

Long Lake is actually an 18-mile, shallow, saline wetland basin. The 16,000-acre basin is defined as a semi-permanent marsh with "edge" expanses of productive seasonally flooded marsh. This "lake" normally has maximum depths of 3-4 feet that can reach up to 7 feet during extended wet periods.

There have been 308 different bird species documented on or adjacent to Long Lake National Wildlife Refuge. Shorebirds are attracted to shallow depths and a meandering shoreline, which provide an essential refueling stop for birds.

Long Lake National Wildlife Refuge

Information

Purchased February 25, 1932; additional land added in August of that year

Size 22,337 acres

Location 1 mile south of Moffit on U.S. Hwy. 83 then 3 miles east on a gravel road (128th Ave)

Features office open 7:30–4, Mon–Friday, includes a lobby, bathrooms, bird list, brochures, map and regulatory information

Facilities wildlife observation area (northwest portion), dock and restrooms (fishing area) and blinds for viewing sharp-tailed grouse in spring

Activities fishing, paddling, boating (25 hp or less), photography, wildlife watching and hunting (pheasant, grouse, partridge and deer). Special seasons regulations apply to fishing and hunting. Contact refuge headquarters for information.

Contact 701-387-4397; longlake@fws.gov; 12000 353rd St SE, Moffit, ND 58560

American white pelicans

HISTORICAL SITES

Whitestone Hill Battlefield State Historic Site

On September 3, 1863, a large gathering of Dakota (Sioux) Indians at a hunting camp were surprised by U.S. Army troops under command of General Alfred Sully.

Despite this group of Dakota not being tied to the New Ulm massacre, a combination of Nebraska and Iowa cavalry attacked the camp of men, women and children with overwhelming force.

As the Dakota attempted to flee, the soldiers killed 150 of them and captured another 300. In this half-hour battle, 20 soldiers were killed and another 38 injured. It marked the start of the Plains Indian War.

Established April 26, 1904. Commemorates both the Dakota Indians and U.S. Army soldiers from the September 3-5 conflict
Location 18 miles southeast of Kulm off of Hwy. 56
Open May 16–Sept 15, Thur–Mon, 10–5
Admission free, donations welcome
Features museum, restroom facilities, on-site parking, playground, picnic and camping area nearby, stone markers and limited accessibility

Museum at Whitestone Battlefield State Historical Site

Ludwig and Christina Welk Farmstead

Before becoming the famous Champagne Music Maker, Lawrence Welk grew up on his parents' farmstead along with eight siblings. His father, Ludwig, immigrated to America in 1892 with his wife, Christina, after an unhappy life in Russia. Born in 1902, Lawrence spoke only German until age 21 when he moved to Bismarck. Welk played his accordion at weddings and dances until 1955, when he made his first appearance on national TV.

Today the original family farmstead—made of 3-foot-thick sod walls and covered by white siding—is open to the public daily from May 15 through September 15 or by appointment. The Welk Farmstead was fully restored in 1992, the year Lawrence died. On an annual basis over 7,000 fans visit the site and take in additional German-Russian festivals and sites.

Contact 701-336-7519

Jamestown

Whether you are traveling to the east or west along I-94 through Jamestown it isn't hard to spot the world's largest buffalo Sitting next to the National Buffalo Museum and Frontier Village, this massive concrete structure is a favorite of children. Known as the "Pride of the Prairie," Jamestown is located halfway between Fargo and Bismarck, the state's capital city. Cruising along the rolling Great Plains you will come to this city of 15,527 as the landscape gives way to the river valleys of the James and Pipestem.

World's Largest Buffalo

Location east of I-94 and U.S. Hwy. 281 junction
Built 1959
Size 60 tons, 26 feet tall
Visitors 150,000-plus annually
Facilities National Buffalo Museum and Frontier Village
Check Out White Cloud, a certified albino buffalo

World's largest buffalo statue

National Buffalo Museum

This history center tells the story of the American bison with a large selection of displays and artifacts. Visitors will learn how this noble beast, commonly known as the buffalo, has evolved over thousands of years.

Hours year-round; summer 9–8; call for winter hours
Admission subject to change
Facilities museum and gift shop
Contact 1-800-807-1511 or 1-701-252-8648
Operated by North Dakota Buffalo Foundation

Bison

Frontier Village

Historical buildings tell the story of how the early pioneers lived on the wide-open prairie landscape.

Features post office, trading post, 1881 church, fire station and barber shop
Hours June–August, 9–9; May–Sept, 10–5
Admission free

Check Out

- Louis L'Amour Trail
- Fort Seward Historic Site and Interpretive Center
- Pipestem Dam and Lake
- Louis L'Amour Gallery and The Arts Center
- The 1914 Basilica of St. James
- North Dakota Sports Hall of Fame

Frontier Village

NORTH DAKOTA STATE PARK SERIES

DOYLE MEMORIAL STATE PARK

INTRODUCTION

A small prairie park of only 21 acres, Doyle Memorial is another of North Dakota's oldest parks. Located on the shoreline of Green Lake, it was admitted into the state park system in 1925. The original acreage was donated by J.J. Doyle, who homesteaded near here with his father in 1884.

Today the park is leased by the city of Wishek and is a popular spot for camping, fishing and boating. Sitting on a peninsula, the park offers numerous places to fish from shore and numerous shelters to host a picnic. Other features include a modern campground, playground and boat ramp.

Entrance to Doyle Memorial Park

Green Lake is a part of the rolling prairie landscape and surrounded by the farmland of south-central North Dakota. The result of a moraine, this shallow lake is a by-product of the great Wisconsinan glaciation thousands of years ago. This area of North Dakota was settled by numerous ethnic groups, including a large number of German-Russians. J.J. Doyle and his father were part of the first wave of settlers and established a homestead 9 miles south of Wishek. As a member of this new community, Doyle served on its first village board in 1898 and later in the North Dakota House of Representatives in 1909 and 1915.

After its creation in the early 1920s, Doyle Memorial became a popular recreational spot for the local community. In the 1940s, as the country focused on World War II, area residents lost interest in the park and it fell into disrepair. Fortunately, a series of major developments and improvements were completed at Doyle Memorial during the 1960s. Help came from the North Dakota National Guard, a matching grant from the Bureau of Outdoor Recreation and leadership from the Wishek Wildlife Club.

If you're looking for a unique German-Russian experience, check out the town of Wishek, located just a few miles from Doyle Memorial State Recreation Area. Wishek hosts numerous festivals honoring this ethnic group with the highlight being Sauerkraut Days. This prairie city also features shops, stores and eating establishments.

Also just down the road is Whitestone Hill Battlefield State Historic Site, a spot that played a major part in North Dakota's early history. It marks an 1863 battle between Dakota Indian tribes and U.S. Army troops. The site also includes a museum and interpretive markers.

Green lake

PARK AT A GLANCE

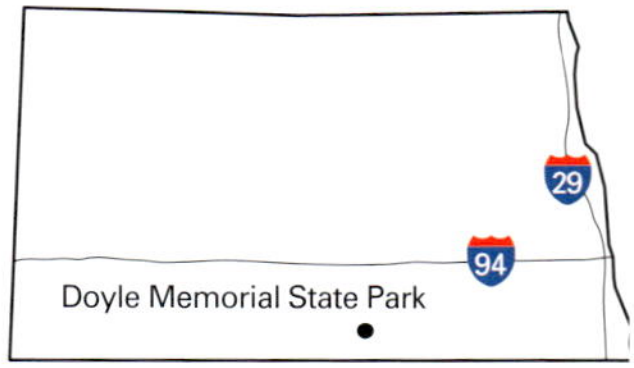

Location/Directions 7 miles southeast of Wishek; 25 miles northwest of Ashley and on the north side of Green Lake.
From Wishek, take Hwy. 13 east for three miles and turn south on 42nd Ave SE for another 4 miles.

Contact Information
Doyle Memorial State Park, Wishek, ND 58495; 701-452-2351; parkrec@nd.gov; ndparks.com/parks/dmsp.htm

Established 1925

Size 21 acres of riparian area and grassland along a large prairie pothole

Visitor Services
- camping
- boat ramp
- picnic shelters
- fishing
- boating
- swimming
- playground
- fish-cleaning station and rock piers

Camping mid-May through Labor Day, 6 RV and tent sites

Things You'll Want To Do

- Camp under the swaying cottonwoods, have a picnic, or go for a swim at the park's beach.
- Go for a slow cruise on Green Lake and check out the diverse wildlife. Or try your luck at fishing for northern pike on the pier.

GETTING TO KNOW THE PARK

GREEN LAKE

- this shallow prairie lake is a good spot to try your hand at fishing, especially for northern pike
- concrete boat ramp located at the east end of the park, also a courtesy dock for launching boats
- fish cleaning station near boat ramp
- Doyle Memorial features numerous spots for fishing from shore, including a dock and long rock pier
- Contact: Wishek Wildlife Club (701) 452-2782

Fishing pier

CAMPING

- 6 RV and tent sites
- 30-amp electrical hookups
- 1 comfort station with showers and flush toilets
- full service Memorial Day Weekend through Labor Day Weekend
- located in a grove of large cottonwood trees and near a sheltered bay of Green Lake

Campground

Additional Features

- playground
- a number of picnic shelters for events or family gatherings
- open space for games
- perfect views of Green Lake

Courtesy dock and boat ramp

INDEX

J

L

M

N

P

R

S

V

W

NOTES

NOTES

NOTES

NOTES

ABOUT THE AUTHOR

Everyone should learn something from their 2-year-old niece. Jenny reminded Scott why it is good to go with the flow of the wind (she loved to run with the wind but hated going against it). This is how he became a park ranger and stuck with it for almost 15 years. Scott discovered the wonderful world of wetlands at Lake Metigoshe and fell into a new career of advocating the need to restore, improve and protect our natural environment. Today Scott is lucky to have a job where one day can mean macroinvertebrate sampling to determine water quality or teaching children of all ages the importance of watershed boundaries or exploring rivers by paddling with a diverse collection of experts. As a result of the winds blowing him east, Scott and his partner and best friend, Angie, now live in southern Minnesota and enjoy going on new adventures wherever the breeze might push them.

Jenny and Scott at Cross Ranch State Park